LIVING PRAYERS FOR TODAY

LIVING PRAYERS FOR TODAY

An anthology of prayers for many occasions

Compiled by
Maureen Edwards

International Bible Reading Association

Cover photograph – Ffotograph – Cardiff
Editor – Maureen Edwards

Published by:
International Bible Reading Association
1020 Bristol Road
Selly Oak
Birmingham B29 6LB
Great Britain

British Library Cataloguing-in-Publication data:
A catalogue record for this book is available from the British Library

ISBN 0-7197-0871-0

First published 1996

© 1996 International Bible Reading Association

Design/Typeset by Avonset, Midsomer Norton, nr Bath
Printed and bound in Great Britain

CONTENTS

PREFACE

A COMMUNITY OF PRAYER

There is a sense in which, although we often seem to pray in isolation from others, we never actually pray alone. Jesus said, 'When you pray, say *Our* Father ...' Prayer instantaneously joins us with others. In ways beyond our understanding, our prayers transcend social, racial and geographical boundaries and become part of a great network of prayer being offered to our loving God who created and sustains us all. Together then we pray for *our* daily bread, for the forgiveness of *our* sin and that *we* may be delivered from evil. Prayer is never purely personal, even if we try to make it so.

Prayer binds us to one another. On a visit to churches in Myanmar (formerly known as Burma) in 1988, many of their members said to me, 'Ask people in Britain to pray for us, and know that we also pray for you.' Although the country has been closed to Christian mission partners since 1966, prayer has a resilience that defies political boundaries, and even death.

LIVING PRAYERS

It broadens our vision when we use prayers from people of other cultures, the young and the elderly, whose insights are different from ours: their words have a freshness that speaks to us. This is a partnership which brings mutual support, and which is not limited to the here and now, but extends back through the generations: the great prayers of the past are alive with meaning and continue to help us to express thoughts and feelings we cannot put into words.

THE STILL SMALL VOICE

Although this book contains many written prayers, words are not always necessary; we know that the Spirit takes up our unspoken prayers and that our silence and sense of emptiness before God become channels through which God speaks to us and renews us.

MANY WAYS

We do not all pray in the same way. Some prayers in this anthology, for example, are more meditative than others. Some may not even sound like formal prayers, but provide a starting-point for reflection and prayer. Some people prefer no other aid to prayer than the Bible and a book of prayers, while others may be helped by lighting candles, or by focusing on other objects. I hope there is something here for everyone.

WHOLENESS

I do not believe in a spirituality that separates itself from the stuff of everyday life and from contemporary issues, and this has influenced the way the prayers are grouped. I am aware that sometimes the themes overlap, but the headings are to help you to select prayers for particular situations. And we hope the index at the end will help you to do this in more detail.

I am deeply grateful to friends and former colleagues who have helped by writing prayers, or by sending prayers from other sources. Selecting a collection of prayers, reading them several times to take them through the various processes of publishing, is for me a privilege – another chance to set aside time to absorb the insights they contain, their profound sense of God's presence and the challenges that arise out of their concern for others and for justice and peace in God's world. May this experience be yours as well.

Maureen Edwards, February 1995

RENEWAL –
DISCOVERING FAITH

GOD is rich in mercy, and because of his great love for us, he brought us to life with Christ when we were dead because of our sins; it is by grace you are saved. And he raised us up in union with Christ Jesus and enthroned us with him in the heavenly realms, so that he might display in the ages to come how immense are the resources of his grace, and how great his kindness to us in Christ Jesus. For it is by his grace you are saved through faith; it is not your own doing. It is God's gift, not a reward for work done. There is nothing for anyone to boast of; we are God's handiwork, created in Christ Jesus for the life of good deeds which God designed for us.

Ephesians 2.4-10 (Revised English Bible)

Something to do and think about

❖ *Make a list of times in your life when you have been most aware of God's presence and have discovered faith.*

❖ *Reflect on each experience and give thanks.*

In search of God

1

Hear me,
from the sky above
where you stay,
from the sea below where you are.
Creator of the world,
potter,
Lord of Lords,
my eyes long to see you.
I long to know you
because in seeing you,
knowing you,
thinking of you,
understanding you,
you will see me and will know me.
The sun, the moon,
the day,
the night,
the summer,
the winter,
do not walk in vain.
They are orderly,
and walk to the determined place
and arrive successfully.
Everywhere you go,
you carry with you
your king's sceptre.
Hear me,
listen to me,
lest I tire,
lest I die.

Prayer of the Incas, Peru

Drawn to God

2 O God, beauty of the day, heart of the heavens and of the earth; giver of wealth, giver of daughters and of sons.

Help us to feel within ourselves the need to search for you, to invoke your name, to praise you along the roads, in the valleys, in the ravines, on the riverbanks, and under the trees.

Protect us that we may not be entangled in evil, that we will not trip into shame and misfortune. Help us not to slip and get hurt, that we may not fall along the way. Protect us from obstacles that might pursue us or appear before us. Give us only beautiful straight paths, beautiful good paths.

Grant that we might believe in you, be drawn to you, and that our existence might be happy. O God, heart of the heavens and of the earth, hidden treasure. You fill the heavens and earth at the four cardinal points. Grant that there might be only peace and tranquillity in the universe, before you, O God. May it be so.

From the Popul Vuh – Mayan book of the Dawn of Life

3 O great God, who art thou? Where art thou? Show thyself to me.

Venkayya, first outcast convert in the Church of South India;
prayer offered every day for three years

4 God, of your goodness give me yourself for you are sufficient for me. I cannot properly ask anything less, to be worthy of you. If I were to ask less, I should always be in want. In you alone do I have all.

Julian of Norwich (1342-1443)

God comes to meet us

5   Lord, you created every part of us
and know and love us completely.
You read our thoughts
and understand every feeling.
When we turn away, you follow,
searching, calling us back,
never put off by our refusal to listen
and turn again.
There is no escape from your presence.
The darkness is not dark enough
to hide from you.

We need to surrender ourselves to you,
to be cleansed by your love
and forgiven over and over again.
Your love is not earned:
it is unconditional,
freely given.
You leave the ninety-nine
and search the world
to find and bring us back.

As we turn to you,
you come running towards us,
embracing us with your love,
ready to protect us with your power.
From stores of goodness,
you adorn us with splendid clothing
to cover our unworthiness.
All that you have is available to us:
    a loving and forgiving spirit,
    joy, peace and tranquillity,
and a wider vision of your Kingdom.

Based on Psalm 139 and Luke 15.11-32
Maureen Edwards

Our desire to love God

6   The more I win thee, Lord,
       the more for thee I pine;
     Ah, such a heart of mine!

     My eyes behold thee, and
         are filled and straightway then
     Their hunger wakes again!

     My arms have clasped thee and
         Should set thee free, but no,
     I cannot let thee go!

     Thou dwell'st within my heart,
         Forthwith anew the fire
     Burns of my soul's desire.

     Lord Jesus Christ, beloved,
         tell, O tell me true,
     What shall thy servant do?

Narayan Vaman Tilak, India (1862-1919)

7   Fortified by faith in your promises,
     Anchored by hope in your resurrected life,
     Embraced by love in your steadfast faithfulness,
         Take my hand, O Lord,
         For there is no other, but you.

Lesley Anderson, Panama

8   O Lord our God, grant us grace to desire thee with our whole heart, that
     so desiring, we may seek and find thee; and so finding thee we may
     love thee; and loving thee we may hate those sins from which thou hast
     redeemed us; for the sake of Jesus Christ.

St Anselm (1033-1109)

Praise God who comes in Christ

9   God of creation,
     God in creation,
     God dwelling in people
     (Your peak of creation)
     We offer You praise.

     How God, can we know You?
     Love, honour, adore You?
     Approach and enjoy You?
     We needed a teacher,
     A human revealer,
     To show us, Creator,
     A pathway to reach You.

     It was Jesus You sent us
     A human-faced Jesus,
     And we see in this Jesus
     What You mean us to be.
     He lived much as we do.
     He died as shall we,
     But his death was different –
     A mystery to me.

     He carried the cross-bar
     He was nailed to the tree,
     'Father, forgive them,'
     That's the world, and that's me.
     He died on the Cross there
     For all to see,
     His arms stretched wide open,
     Linking You, God – with me.

     But death couldn't hold him.
     His Spirit is free.
     Offering friendship for ever
     To all – Yes, to me!

Hilda Stephenson

6

Discover the gentleness of God

10 A missionary in Nigeria poses the riddle: 'When is a knee almost like an elephant?' He goes on to explain that in the Hausa language the word for knee is very similar to that for 'elephant', and tells of the preacher whose grasp of Hausa was not outstanding, and who, in reference to Philippians 2.10 delivered a sermon on how even elephants will bow the knee to Christ!

Likewise, Lord Jesus,
whether by error or in jest
may all our ungainliness and blundering
lead us to your feet.

John Carden

11 God of surprises, give us grace and courage
to stoop low enough, that we may find heaven there.

Simon Barrow

12 I come before the God of disclosure and honesty,
who calls me to truth in Christ, whose Spirit is unafraid.
I come before the God of selflessness,
gentleness and patience
who will be selfless, gentle and patient with me.

Lavinia Byrne

God accepts us

13 O Living God,
you call us to yourself.

From the fullness,
or the emptiness, of our daily lives
you cry out to us.
In the moan of pain,
and in the shout of laughter,
you are present.

As we seek to respond to our joys and sorrows
with love and penitence,
faith and thankfulness,
you embrace us.

Hear our sorrow, O God of mercy,
for our falling short of your high love,
our unwillingness to entrust our hopes and dreams to you,
our resistance to your encircling arms.

May we draw from you courage,
because you accept us;
faith, because you understand us;
hope, because you believe in us;
and love, because you will to love through us,
this day and forever. Amen

Julie Hulme

14 O wondrous, amazing, lovely God,
beautiful and loving beyond compare:
come to us now as we stand bewildered and alone,
and fill our lonely hearts to overflowing.

Sheila Cassidy

We find new meaning

15 Creator God, you are light:
there is no darkness in you.
Before the heat and strife of day,
in the stillness,
we rise to meditate and pray.
Gently lead us
out of darkness,
bitterness and despair
into the dawn
of enlightenment and reconciliation.

Written in Sri Lanka, 1988
Maureen Edwards

16 Rejoice, people of God!
Celebrate the life within you,
and Christ's presence in your midst!

Our eyes shall be opened!
The present will have new meaning,
and the future will be bright with hope.

Rejoice, people of God!
Bow your heads before the One
who is our wisdom and our strength.

We place ourselves before our God.
That we may be touched and cleansed
by the power of God's Spirit.

Methodist Church in Guatemala

We are sent out

17 Go now, believing in God the Creator Spirit,
who moved upon the face of the deep
at the beginning of creation,
who created all that is
and who spoke through the prophets of old.

Go, trusting in Jesus Christ,
in whom God's Spirit was poured
in the fullness of time,
in whom the whole creation is restored,
and who promised that the Spirit would come
to empower the faithful to witness
to the mighty love of God.

Go, forth in the power of the Holy Spirit
to witness to God's love in Christ,
and to proclaim with words and deeds
the good news of love and hope
for all humankind and the world.

**Glory be to God – Creator, Christ and the Holy Spirit –
now and always! Amen**

Salvador T Martinez, Thailand

RENEWAL –
GROWING IN FAITH

ITH this in mind, then, I kneel in prayer to the Father, from whom every family in heaven and on earth takes its name, that out of the treasures of his glory he may grant you inward strength and power through his Spirit, that through faith Christ may dwell in your hearts in love. With deep roots and firm foundations may you, in company with all God's people, be strong to grasp what is the breadth and length and height and depth of Christ's love, and to know it, though it is beyond knowledge. So may you be filled with the very fullness of God.

Now to him who is able through the power which is at work among us to do immeasurably more than we can ask or conceive, to him be glory in the church and in Christ Jesus from generation to generation for evermore! Amen.

Ephesians 3. 14-21 (Revised English Bible)

Something to do and think about

❖ *If you made the list suggested on page 1, write by the side of each experience what you learnt about God. Where has your faith been deepened and strengthened most?*

❖ *Do you have a record of music associated with any of these experiences? Listen to it when you pray some of these prayers.*

Call to worship

18 God who is beyond all our naming
and all our defining,
God from whose being flows creative diversity
and who is the source of our unity: **We worship you.**

God who was born into the depths of our life,
who entered our history in Christ,
enfleshed in the midst of every culture,
incarnate in every struggle for truth: **We worship you.**

Spirit of God who dances free of us all,
calling us past boundaries
of race, gender, culture, system and nation: **We worship you.**
   We approach you in faith
   held fast by your love for the whole creation.

World Council of Churches

19 We believe in God who loves us
and wants us to love each other.
This is our God.
We believe in Jesus who cared
about children and held them in his arms.
He wanted a world where everyone
could live together in peace.
This is Jesus Christ.
We believe in the Holy Spirit who
keeps working with us until
everything is good and true.
This is the Holy Spirit.
We can be the church which reminds
people of God because we love each other.
This we believe.

Prepared by children for the World Council of Churches' Assembly in Canberra,
1991

That we may become like Christ

20 Grant me, O God,
    the heart of a child,
pure and transparent as a spring;
    a simple heart,
which never harbours sorrows;
a heart glorious in self-giving,
    tender in compassion;
a heart faithful and generous,
which will never forget any good
or bear a grudge for any evil.

Make me a heart gentle and humble,
    loving without asking any return,
    large-hearted and undauntable,
which no ingratitude can sour
and no indifference can weary;
    a heart penetrated by the love of Jesus
    whose desire will only be satisfied in heaven.

Grant me O Lord,
    the mind and heart
    of thy dear Son.

George Appleton

21 Eternal God, you are surrounded by the light of heavenly splendour;
grant us so to celebrate the truth of your Gospel that we may see your
glory in the face of Jesus Christ. Amen

Norman Wallwork

We confess

22 O Lord, our Father, we are always putting up barriers.
Barriers around our thoughts;
we certainly want to keep some of those hidden,
even from you, if we can.
Break down those barriers, Lord,
cleanse the dark corners of our minds,
so that we have nothing to hide
and can be open to you, and to others.

Barriers around our hearts;
we don't want to let too many people come too close;
we want to be sparing with our love
lest people get too demanding.
Jesus said, 'The amount you measure out
is the amount you will be given.'
Lord, does that apply to love, too?
Ours, and yours?

Barriers around our spirits;
we can barely cope with the world of our senses,
we are too fearful, or too busy
to cope with the world of the Spirit,
so we close it off.
Help us to see, Lord,
that these are not separate worlds.
The world of the senses is insipid, bleak, meaningless,
without the Spirit which enriches, and enlightens it.

So, Lord, I open the gates.
Come in, and make yourself at home;
you'll find that what I was defending isn't much
but such as it is I offer it to you,
for cleansing, healing and empowering with your Spirit.
Glory to you, O Lord, for your forgiving love! Amen

Val Spouge

Lord have mercy

23 In the light of the Spirit and in union with Christ
we acknowledge our failures before God.
Lord, your ways are not our ways:
your thoughts are not our thoughts:
what seems like eternity
is only a moment to you.
In the face of eternity,
help us to be humble.
Lord have mercy upon us.

If we have been singing praises with our voices
and kept the joy out of our hearts;
If we have prayed only for what was possible
and hoped only for what we could see;
Lord have mercy upon us.

If we have taken your grace for granted
and expected instant answers to immediate requests;
If we have allowed waiting on your Spirit to slip into laziness
and waiting on the Kingdom to be replaced by apathy;
If we have only thought of us waiting on you
and never pondered how you wait on us:
Lord have mercy upon us.

Listen, for this is the true word of God
blessed are all who wait for the Lord.
God is merciful, and God's love is sure and strong.
Amen

World Council of Churches

Faith grows

24 Behold Lord, an empty vessel that needs to be filled. My Lord, fill it. I am weak in the faith; strengthen me. I am cold in love; warm me and make me fervent, that my love may go out to my neighbour. I do not have a strong and firm faith; at times I doubt and am unable to trust you altogether. O Lord, help me. Strengthen my faith and trust in you. Amen

Martin Luther (1483-1546)

25 O God, I know that if I do not love thee with all my heart, with all my mind, with all my soul and with all my strength, I shall love something else with all my heart and mind and soul and strength. Grant that putting thee first in all my lovings I may be liberated from all lesser loves and loyalties, and have thee as my first love, my chiefest good and my final joy.

George Appleton

26 Lord of renewal, help us in the practice of our faith
to recognize those things which are at the heart
of our relationship with you and those which are not.

Michael Townsend

27 Creator God, according to your mighty promises strengthen us in our weakness, grant us light for your path, grace for our trials and help from your holy place; through Jesus Christ our Lord. Amen

Pakistan

28 Father, thank you for knowing me more than I know myself.
Help me to know, to love, to trust you more,
and to grow stronger in you.

Nihar Chhatriya, North India

To be fashioned to a truer beauty

29 O Christ, the Master Carpenter,
who at the last, through wood and nails,
purchased our whole salvation,
wield well your tools in the workshop of your world,
so that we, who come rough-hewn to your bench,
may here be fashioned to a truer beauty of your hand.
We ask it for your name's sake.

Source unknown

30 Christ be with me, Christ before me, Christ behind me,
Christ in me, Christ beneath me, Christ above me,
Christ on my right, Christ on my left,
Christ where I lie, Christ where I sit, Christ where I arise,
Christ in the heart of everyone who thinks of me,
Christ in the mouth of everyone who speaks of me,
Christ in every eye that sees me,
Christ in every ear that hears me.
   Salvation is of the Lord,
   Salvation is of the Lord,
   Salvation is of Christ,
   May your salvation, O Lord, be ever with us.

St Patrick (389-461)

31 Thanks be to thee, O Lord Jesus Christ, for all the benefits which thou
hast given us; for all the pains and insults which thou hast borne for us.
O Most merciful redeemer, friend and brother, may we know thee more
clearly, love thee more dearly, and follow thee more nearly; for thine
own sake.

St Richard of Chichester (1197-1253)

Learning to love

32 O God:
Enlarge my heart
that it may be big enough to receive the greatness of your love.
Stretch my heart
that it may take into it all those who with me around the world
believe in Jesus Christ.
Stretch it
that it may take in all those who do not know him,
but who are my responsibility because I know him.
And stretch it
that it may take in all those who are not lovely in my eyes,
and whose hands I do not want to touch;
through Jesus Christ, my saviour, Amen.

Prayer of an African Christian

Love without hypocrisy

33 Lord, my God
today I have decided to love you
without beating my chest
without change in my pocket
without praying on my knees, down front, in the centre
without daily visits to the church
without hypocritical hymns
without banal words
even without crying out Alleluia!

Lord, my God
together with the children of the market trash collectors
with the shouting children, the fruit vendors, car watchers
with the shoe shiners
with the farmers dispossessed of their lands
with workers who increase the capital of others
with mothers who sell their flesh to buy bread for their children
with the old people left forgotten on the streets
with the mentally retarded
with the anonymous alcoholics of the neighbourhoods
with all the helpless handicapped people
and through them I have decided to love you.

Lord, I have decided to love you
by giving to them that which I have
because what you have given me
is not for myself
but for them.

Orlando Perez V, Nicaragua

34 O God, help me to walk in the boots of the miner, the shoes of the
trader, the moccasins of the trapper, and the sandals of Jesus the
Master. Amen

Native American prayer

19

Courage to choose life

35 Resurrection God,
we want to know ...

We want to know the truth about you,
not so much the obscure things and finer points,
but we want to know if you will still be there for us
all our lives
and when we are dying:
we want to know if your hand will hold us
when we feel we're sinking.
**Teach us your promises,
and give us faith to trust you.**

We want to know the truth about the choices we face:
where is the good and evil in them,
where life and death?
What coffee shall I buy?
What bank shall I use?
Should I stay the night?
Should I offer my house for a homeless person to lodge?
Organ repairs or Christian Aid?
Is it right to have an abortion?
Guide us in your ways.

And where the truth is staring us in the face,
Give us courage to choose life.

We recognize your authority:
we pray now for all who seek to know the truth:
**Guide the people of this world,
and lead us all to life.**

Bob Warricker

God is my strength

36 Because God is, I don't need to fear anyone.
Who should I be afraid of?
God himself is light ...
A light shining and lighting up every shadow and fearful place
inside and out. I can see where I'm going.
When we are afraid,
He makes us strong and confident to go in and out.
God is the unshakeable strength of my life.
He heals and saves and rescues us from fear.

God shelters me under his umbrella.
When troubles fall on me like a thunderstorm ...
and life is too tough.
God hides me away in his tent, while I find my feet,
He shows me that the ground is solid rock,
High up enough to see where I am.

But God, do you hear me?
Listen to my shout for help,
Have pity on me when I cry!
Don't hide yourself from me.
Please show me that you have heard my voice,
and show me how to follow your way of living.

I trust this,
That while I am still on this earth, alive, in this life,
I will see with my own eyes all the goodness of God –
God who wants our life to be worthwhile.

So place your hope in God, who believes in you.
Be strong because God is in you and around you.
Allow yourself to be stronger and bolder, each day
in the company of God.
Put your hope in him and in what he is doing among you.

Based on Psalm 27, David McManus, Hope Community

Growing in confidence

37 Deepen our confidence, O Christ, and increase our faith, that we may live with one another, not as those who have heard of you but as those who are sure of you and not as those who know about you but as those who know you; for your own name's sake. Amen

Leslie Weatherhead (1893-1976)

38 Lord Jesus Christ, friend and saviour of the sinner,
call us away from self-absorption,
from a fearful scrutiny of our own motives,
from all useless anxiety and dread.
Call us to yourself.

Lavinia Byrne

39 Lord Jesus,
Fortify my faith
   In the promises of your cross.
Anchor my hope
   In the certainty of your resurrection.
Emblazon my love
   In the experience of your presence. Amen

Lesley Anderson, Panama

40 Lord, I thank you for those whose influence first led me
into your company.
Show me if there is someone in my immediate circle
to whom I should be particularly commending your call.

Pauline Webb

RENEWAL –
DISCOVERING
WHOLENESS

URGE you, then ... remembering the mercies of God, to offer your bodies as a living sacrifice, dedicated and acceptable to God; that is the kind of worship for you, as sensible people. Do not model your behaviour on the contemporary world, but let the renewing of your minds transform you, so that you may discern for yourselves what is the will of God – what is good and acceptable and mature.

Romans 12.1-2 (New Jerusalem Bible)

Something to do and think about

❖ *Look around your home. Bring together symbols of different aspects of your life: your family, friends, work, hobbies, church, clubs, failures, times of sickness or bereavement, successes, anything that links you with the rest of the world ... Reflect on them as you use these prayers.*

❖ *Draw a diagram to illustrate the interdependence of the mind, body and spirit of the individual with the family, community and the world.*

❖ *What is 'wholeness'?*

Growing towards the light

41 Lord God, clouds have descended
and everything I learnt
in times of certainty
seems hidden.
The mist swirls and envelops all
in an overwhelming sense of unreality,
quiet and sombre,
a ghostly silence,
emphasizing every sound.
Changing impressions,
shapes and thoughts loom up,
feelings of helplessness
and disillusionment.
I grasp after what is there:
your hand,
your presence diffusing the mist,
until the way before me,
in all its detail,
reflects the warmth of your reassuring love.

Maureen Edwards

42 Give me a candle of the Spirit, O God,
As I go down into the deep of my own being.
Show me the hidden things,
Take me down to the spring of my life,
And tell me my nature and name.
Give me freedom to grow
So that I may become the self,
The seed which Thou didst plant at my making
Out of the deep I cry unto Thee, O Lord.

George Appleton

Into the healing presence of God

43 Lead us, O Lord,
from the night of doubt and despair
into the daylight of dialogue and hope.
Lead us out of the tomb of suspicion and fear,
into the life of faith and trust.
Lead us out of the darkness of terror and hate
into the sunlight of security and love;
and lead us out of the gloom of isolation and hurt
into the healing presence of your glory;
through Jesus Christ our Lord. Amen

Norman Wallwork

44 God of power and might and glory, shadow and shade,
give me a sense of my own glory,
made as I am in the image and likeness of your glory,
for your glory and not for shame.
Hide me in your shadow as I seek to know my hidden self,
and then call me out into your merciful light
for the glory of your name.

Lavinia Byrne

45 O Thou great Chief, light a candle in my heart, that I may see what is
therein, and sweep the rubbish from thy dwelling place.

An African schoolgirl

Finding peace

46 O Saviour Christ, we beseech thee, when the wind is boisterous, and our faith weak, and we begin to sink even as we would fain come to thee on the water, stretch forth thy hand, O Lord, as of old to thy fearful disciple, and say to the sea of our difficulties, Peace be still; for thy holy Name's sake.

Dean Vaughan

47 God of love, you watch with all who weep or worry.
You offer hope to those in despair
and your calming presence to the troubled.
Give us peace.

Leta Hawe, New Zealand

48 God of stillness and creative action
Help us to find space for quietness today,
That we may live creatively,
Discover the inner meaning of silence
And learn the wisdom that heals the world.
Send peace and joy to each quiet place,
To all who are waiting and listening.
May your still small voice be heard
Through Christ in the love of the Spirit. Amen

Julie Hulme

49 Deep peace of the Running Water to you,
Deep peace of the Flowing Air to you
Deep peace of the Quiet Earth to you,
Deep peace of the Shining Stars to you,
Deep peace of the Son of Peace to you.

Celtic Blessing

Receiving the Spirit

50 May your Holy Spirit fill me
with the love I need so much.
May your presence never leave me,
may I feel your loving touch.
Holy Jesus, may your Spirit
fill my heart, my soul, my life.

May your goodness overflow me,
may your peace find lodging here.
Take away all doubts and worries,
may I always know you care.
Holy Jesus, may your Spirit
fill my heart, my soul, my life.

May I see you in all faces,
may I never let you down.
Forgive me Lord, if I deny you,
help me share the love I've known.
Holy Jesus, may your Spirit
fill my heart, my soul, my life.

May your shadow fall across me,
liberate this heart of mine.
May I see the face of glory
and know the power of love divine.
Holy Jesus, may your Spirit
fill my heart, my soul, my life.

Maureen Romang

51 Almighty God, unto whom all hearts be open, all desires known, and
from whom no secrets are hid: Cleanse the thoughts of our hearts by
the inspiration of thy Holy Spirit, that we may perfectly love thee, and
worthily magnify thy holy name; through Christ our Lord.

Book of Common Prayer

The wounded healer

52 His wounds are healing wounds;
Which show his love for me.
They penetrate my inward heart:
'All this I did for thee'.

My wounds are part of me,
Healed now, though scars remain;
Forgiven hurts enable me,
Reach others in their pain.

Come, be my welcome guest,
My heart is open wide;
Re-live your hurts in confidence,
The Lord is on your side.

Then go your way in peace,
Your wounds and his combine,
To progress your discipleship,
And cause the sun to shine.

Based on the words of Mother Julian: 'Our wounds can become our worships.'
Howard Booth

53 Tender God,
you have seen my affliction,
and unbound my eyes;
you have bereaved me of the burden
to which I used to cling;
you have woven my pain
into patterns of integrity;
the wounds I cherished
you have turned into honours,
and the scars I kept hidden
into marks of truth.
You have touched me gently;
I have seen your face, and live.

Janet Morley

Recognizing wholeness

54 I asked for strength that I might achieve;
I was made weak that I might learn humbly to obey.

I asked for health that I might do greater things;
I was given infirmity that I might do better things.

I asked for riches that I might be happy;
I was given poverty that I might be wise.

I asked for power that I might have the praise of others;
I was given weakness that I might feel the need of God.

I asked for all things that I might enjoy life;
I was given life that I might enjoy all things.

I got nothing that I had asked for,
but everything that I had hoped for.

Almost despite myself my unspoken prayers were answered;
I am ... most richly blessed.

Prayer of an unknown Confederate soldier

55 God, who has chosen the weak and the foolish,
help me to be glad that I am one of them.
Save me from false pretensions or delusions of grandeur
and teach me that your grace is sufficient for me,
that your strength is made perfect in my weakness.

Pauline Webb

Peace and wholeness

56 I weave a silence to my lips ...
　　　　my mind ...
　　　　my heart ...
Calm me, O Lord,
as you stilled the storm.
Still me, O Lord,
keep me from harm.
Let all the tumult
within me cease.
Enfold me, Lord,
in your peace.

Based on a Gaelic prayer
Peter Millar

57 Lord, forgive us,
for we are fragmented persons.
We go many directions at once.
We seek opposite goals;
we serve contradictory causes.
We mouth liberation, we live oppression.
We shout peace, we practise
violence and anarchy.
We shout justice, we walk in injustice.
We preach love, we practise hate.
Through your compassion
have mercy on us and make us whole.
Enable us to discern your voice
among the dissonant voices.

The Philippines

Abundant life

58 Lord, you have come
to offer us
abundant life
rich
overflowing
energetic
and exciting.

When our lives are tired
and our spirits stagnate
come to us with your resources
of humour and hope
lest
in lukewarm sadness
we forget your power.

When we become
cotton-wool Christians
softened by age or wealth,
grasp us with the urgency of your gospel
lest
in feeble cowardice
we deny your resurrection.

When our gifts remain unoffered
and our talents unused
expose our light
to the darkness of the world
lest
in needless fear
we flicker and die.

Lord, we offer back to you
abundant life
rich
overflowing
energetic
and exciting.

David Jenkins

For the good of all

59 There's a time for healing,
and a time for forgiving.
There's a time for building bridges,
and that time is now.
Oh take our hearts Lord,
take our minds.
Take our hands Lord
and make them one.

From a banner in St George's Cathedral, Jerusalem

60 Forgiving God, help me to be forgiving too.
Show me how I may begin to mend broken relationships;
and strengthen those who find it difficult to forgive.
Help me to resist the temptation to be popular
rather than taking the harder path of doing your will.

Lesley Husselbee

61 O Lord give me strength to refrain from the unkind silence that is born of hardness of heart; the unkind silence that clouds the serenity of understanding and is the enemy of peace.

Give me strength to be the first to tender the healing word and the renewal of friendship, that the bonds of amity and the flow of charity may be strengthened for the good of (all) and the furthering of thine eternal, loving purpose.

Cecil Hunt

Becoming God's servants in the world

62 Lord, you promise to heal the blind,
but I fear what I might see.
By the power of your disturbing Spirit,
help me to claim the miracle
that I may see as you see,
face the fear of your judgment
and, accepting your forgiveness,
be your servant in the world.

Mary Cotes

63 Let the stream of God's love flow among us
We will draw from it
Let the fire of God's love flame within us
We will nourish it
Let the bread of God's providing shower upon us
We will feed on it
Let the wind of God's spirit stir around us
We will be moved by it
Let the arms of God's mercy enfold us
We will share the embracing
Let the dove of God's peace be a guide to us
We will follow it.

Julie Hulme

Becoming part of a larger wholeness

64 I believe in one world, full of riches meant for
everyone to enjoy;
I believe in one race, the family of mankind, learning
how to live together by the hard way of self-sacrifice.
I believe in one life, exciting and positive;
which enjoys all the beauty, integrity and science;
uses the discipline of work to enrich society;
harmonizes with the life of Jesus,
and develops into a total joy.
I believe in one morality: love –
the holiness of sharing the sorrow and joys
of others;
bringing together people as true friends;
working to rid the world of the root causes of poverty
and injustice, ignorance and fear;
love, the test of all my thoughts and motives;
love, guiding me, controlling me, assuring me of
God's forgiveness;
and giving me confidence under his Spirit's control.
I believe in Jesus, and the Bible's evidence about him;
whose life, death and resurrection prove God's
lasting love for the world;
who combines in himself, life, love, truth,
humanity, reality
and God;
who saves, guides, and unites all people who
follow his way.
I believe in the purpose of God,
to unite in Christ everything, spiritual or secular,
to renew society, individuals and nations,
and to guide all governments under his fatherly
direction.

Indian National Industrial Mission

RENEWAL –
PILGRIMAGE

LESSED are the poor in spirit;
the kingdom of Heaven is theirs.
Blessed are the sorrowful;
they shall find their consolation.
Blessed are the gentle;
they shall have the earth for their possession.
Blessed are those who hunger and thirst to see right prevail;
they shall be satisfied.
Blessed are those who show mercy;
mercy shall be shown to them.
Blessed are those whose hearts are pure;
they shall see God.
Blessed are the peacemakers;
they shall be called God's children.
Blessed are those who are persecuted in the cause of right;
the kingdom of Heaven is theirs.

Matthew 5.3-10 (Revised English Bible)

Something to do and think about

❖ *Draw a map to symbolize your journey through life so far, and to indicate what may lie ahead. Mark the points which have meant most to you. When did you set off in new directions? How has your outlook on the world developed and what changes of lifestyle have you made along the way?*

❖ *What is your goal – your vision of God's Kingdom? What challenges does this make to you now?*

The journey so far

65 *The Bible contains some powerful stories of journeys – Abraham setting out from Haran, the Exodus, Jesus' journey to Jerusalem and the Cross, Paul's travels. They are also stories about the human experience of God. Each of us has a story of our own journey which may have taken us a long way through life, even if we have only travelled a few miles. As we reflect on our journey let us*
thank God for good times, places and people;
say sorry to God for what we did, thought or said;
ask God to heal painful memories and broken relationships.

Think back to your earliest memory.

Silence

Think back to your childhood.

Silence

Think back to your schooldays ...

Silence

Depending on where you – and others with whom you may be praying – are on your journey, continue through the stages of your life.

Lord, as I look back on the journey of my life
    help me accept myself as I am and let you love me;
    to be thankful for all that is good in what I have remembered;
    to recognize where I have failed and accept your forgiveness;
    to live in love and care for others.

Father, call me forward into whatever lies ahead
    as you called Abraham.
Jesus, walk the road with me
    as you travelled with your disciples towards Emmaus.
Spirit, inspire and equip me
    as you did with Paul.
May I never cease travelling
    until I reach the journey's end in you, Lord.

Simon Oxley

God has been with us

66 Lord, as I look back on the journey so far, I see how Thy love and
Thy goodness have been with me, through many failings and
angers, in many joys and adventures. I have received much love from
friends, enjoyed so many good and lovely things, been guided and
inspired by the wisdom and encouragement of many teachers and
writers.
Often I have felt Thy presence near, and often I have had to walk
by faith.
Forgive my slowness, my failures in faith, the smallness of my
love, my poor use of Thy grace.
Accept my heart's thanks for growing knowledge of Thee, for
increasing assurances of Thy purposes of love and deepening
knowledge of the things that are eternal. As I turn again to the
journey ahead, it is bright with Thy mercies of the past, dear God
and Saviour.

George Appleton

67 Unless thou lead me, Lord,
the road I journey is all too hard.
Through trust in thee alone
can I go on.

Toyohiko Kagawa, Japan

68 Almighty God, whose kingdom is for the poor in Spirit, and whose best
provision for your chosen people is a tent and a pilgrim staff; grant that
we look not for permanence in the work of human hands, nor seek
safety other than in the company of that Wayfarer who had nowhere to
lay his head, even your Son Jesus Christ our Lord.

Church Missionary Society

Travelling on

69 Grant to us, O Lord, light adequate for each stage of our journey,
companions enough to brighten our way and grace sufficient for our
pilgrimage through time into eternity; through Christ our Lord. Amen

Norman Wallwork

70 Loving God, you have called us to set out on our pilgrimage in faith.
Help us to travel on with you in hope, sharing your love with all those
whom we meet, until together we come to the place where you wait to
welcome all your beloved children; through the one who is the Way,
Jesus Christ our Lord. Amen

Susan Howdle

71 O Light in dark, shine on.
Reveal the open footpath, step by step,
and scatter fear, confusion, hate,
that I may be consumed
by love alone.

O Dark in light, surround
my way, embrace my stumbling, warm the shades,
and so enfold bewilderment
and doubt that faith, like clouds,
may bear me home.

Julie Hulme

We are a pilgrim people

72 By the grace of God we are a pilgrim people, ever moving forward and never settling down with the status quo. We bring our commitment to unity and mission, sharing with all the fullness of the blessing of the good news of Jesus Christ.
Holy God, fill us with the power of your Spirit that we may be your witnesses to the ends of the earth. Amen

Church of South India

73 *The journey blessing*

Bless to me, O God,
The earth beneath my foot,
Bless to me, O God,
The path whereon I go;
Bless to me, O God,
The thing of my desire;
Thou Evermore of evermore,
Bless Thou to me my rest.

Bless to me the thing
Whereon is set my mind,
Bless to me the thing
Whereon is set my love;
Bless to me the thing
Whereon is set my hope;
O Thou King of kings,
Bless Thou to me mine eye!

Scottish traditional

The way of the servant

74 Lord Jesus, you chose the way
of suffering and service
and called us to follow,
not seeking to dominate others,
but discovering the power of love
through sharing with the poor
in their struggle for justice.
Those who follow this way
are ridiculed,
subjected to every conceivable indignity.
They are tortured,
unjustly sentenced to death,
targets of the assassin's bullet,
often to the dumb amazement
of the nation's
and the world's spectators.

This demonstration of integrity,
an unquenchable flame,
which comes from being filled with God's Spirit,
cuts through pretence
and proclaims a message
more penetrating than any words;
it makes the gospel credible;
it is the light for which the world is waiting;
its influence reaches the farthest islands.

Holy Spirit,
strengthen our commitment
to follow the way of the Servant,
and to share in your mission to the world,
when it is costly to do so. Amen

Based on Isaiah 42.1-4
Maureen Edwards

Questions in the wilderness

75 Creator God –
you made this diverse, dangerous, dancing universe:
fireballs among the planets, and glow-worms,
whales and plankton,
ancient rocks and blades of new grass,
infinite numbers of stars, snowflakes, grains of sand,
the desert and the river running through,
the withering wind and springs from deep in the earth.
Why finds no answer, words fail –
yet we praise you.

Crucified God –
you hang on the tree of life,
which we have tried to make a tree of death.
All around, creatures multiply
and people try to subdue the earth;
there is a feast of plenty, and a learning of the law;
injustice is challenged,
and yet people are still suffering in stormy seas
and turbulent societies.
So much pain. Why? Why?
Why finds no answer, words fail –
yet we praise you.

Companion God –
You are always with us, in good times and bad
beside still waters, and in the barren wilderness
you are above, shielding us,
below, upholding us,
beside, encouraging us,
behind, challenging us,
before, guiding us.
You are always travelling on, calling us to follow.
Why finds no answer, words fail –
yet we praise you.

Caring God –
you know our needs;
you feel our hunger and thirst:
when we hunger to understand more,
when we thirst for your Spirit to flow
through dry worship and dying hopes, you are there:
offering bread for the journey,
letting living water flow.
Why finds no answer, words fail –
yet we praise you. Amen

Jan S Pickard

Call us back into the desert

76 Lord our God,
trembling,
we dare to ask
that you call us
into the desert
where we may once more hear you
whisper our name with love.

Sheila Cassidy

77 Suffer me never to think that I have knowledge enough to need no
teaching, wisdom enough to need no correction, talents enough to
need no grace, goodness enough to need no progress, humility enough
to need no repentance, devotion enough to need no quickening,
strength sufficient without thy Spirit: lest, standing still, I fall back for
evermore.

Eric Milner-White (1884-1964)

Our feet are dirty

78 Lord, your disciples are coming to you.
Our feet are dirty from the paths we have trodden.
Our hearts are hungry for you.
Wash us, Lord,
Feed us with your love:
Unite us with Christ,
Give us hope for the world.

Our feet are dirty
from the paths of everyday life,
from making the wrong compromises
when faced with important decisions,
from not giving time or energy
to those whom we need and love,
from running fast to get away from you
or dawdling in the hope of being left behind!
Our hearts are hungry for you,
for the assurance of knowing we are loved,
for the belief there is a purpose in life.
We need: the peace,
          the strength,
          the joy,
     that come from you.
Wash us, Lord,
Feed us with your love:
Unite us with Christ,
Give us hope for the world.

Our feet are dirty
from the paths of suffering;
the experience and knowledge of pain
clings to us and darkens our lives.
Illness, starvation, natural disaster,
bereavement, handicaps, war ...
the stones on life's path
cause us to bleed.

Our hearts are hungry for you,
for the bread and wine we share together,
symbols of the suffering you share with us.
We need: the courage,
          the compassion,
          the faith,
     that come from you.

Wash us, Lord,
Feed us with your love:
Unite us with Christ,
Give us hope for the world.

Our feet are dirty
from the ways of the world,
from standing idly by:
while injustice and oppression
besmirch so many lands;
while the wealthy exploit the poor
who lie down hungry in the dust to die.
Our hearts are hungry for you,
for the sacrifice of your love
that leads us into your kingdom.
We need: the wisdom,
        the justice,
        the love,
    that come from you.

Wash us, Lord,
Feed us with your love:
Unite us with Christ,
Give us hope for the world.

In the name of Christ
   the Living Water,
   the Bread of Life,
   the True Vine, Amen

Christine Odell

That we may walk and not faint

79 O my Lord and God
    the journey is too great for me
  unless
     thou feed me with bread from heaven
      and wine of life
  unless
     thou share with me thine own life
      victorious over sin,
      hatred, pain, and death.
Let thy blood
  flow through my veins
  thy strength
  be my strength
  thy love
  be my love
  And the father's will
  be my will as well as thine
Let me be one with thee
  in heart, mind, and will.

George Appleton

80 Lord, we thank you for all who lift our spirits, so that we feel able to mount up with wings as eagles, to run and not be weary, to walk and not faint. Show us how we too can encourage others, particularly when they are finding the going hard. May we help them to find refreshment of body and peace of mind, for your name's sake.

Pauline Webb

We are not defeated

81 Father God, hold us tight.
Lift us on to your shoulders,
so that we may rest awhile
for the going is rough
and we are very tired.

Sheila Cassidy

82 Lord,
When our steps are weary
And the going is rough
When our life is dreary
And our journey is tough
Open the gate of glory

Lord,
When the dark clouds thicken
And the storm rides high
When the troubles quicken
And danger is nigh
Open the gate of glory

Lord,
When our work is completed
And the battle is done
We are not defeated
The victory you have won
Open the gate of glory

In the Celtic tradition, David Adams

The Spirit leads

83 O Spirit of Life
brooding over the waters of our chaos,
engendering order,
bringing forth light,
discerning and discovering life:
we adore you.
In you is the fountain of life:
In your light do we see light.

O Spirit of life,
welling as a spring within us,
quenching our thirst,
flooding in worship,
flowing in grace:
we adore you.
In you is the fountain of life:
In your light do we see light.

O Spirit of Life,
present with us in truth on the way,
speaking from our tradition,
nourishing our dreams,
leading us in adventure:
we adore you.
In you is the fountain of life:
In your light do we see light.

O Spirit of Life,
wild as the wind in high places,
breaking the walls of our love,
bursting our categories of hope,
carrying us beyond sight into faith:
we adore you.
In you is the fountain of life:
In your light do we see light.

O Spirit of Life,
merciful love of the Father,
compassionate service of Christ,
untamed communion of God with us:
gentle us in believing,
unsettle our certainties,
and strengthen us in the truth
in which we are held,
this day and forever. Amen

Julie Hulme

Stretch our hearts and minds

84 Father God, Lord of the universe,
stretch our hearts and minds,
for we are only little people.
Fearful and conservative,
we seek a smooth path to a safe and cosy God,
who will keep us warm forever.
Blow our minds with your mighty word,
so that one day we may dare
to accept and return your jealous love.

Sheila Cassidy

85 O God of pilgrimage and covenant, grant us the faith to stay with you as
you travel on; that amid changes that leave the mind bewildered,
anxieties that wear away our strength, and hopes deferred that make
the heart sick, we may never doubt the triumph of your love while He
who is the Way, the Truth and the Life is ever illuminating the path
before us, even Jesus Christ our Lord.

Church Missionary Society

Help us to take risks

86 Come, Lord, with us
and help us to cross the sea
that blocks our way to live with peace and justice.

Magali do Nascimento Cunha, Brazil

87 Lord, thank you for the 'new exodus'
that began at Jerusalem.
Help me to participate in your new liberating acts
in my own community
and wherever possible in other parts of my country
and the world.

M Gnanavaram, South India

88 Disturb the complacency of my life, O God
and help me with the passing years
to become ever more ready to learn new truths
and to risk new ventures of faith.

Pauline Webb

In the land of the cross

89 O God,
I came to your holy land, like Moses to the desert,
seeking a pure encounter,
a cleansing, a pilgrimage,
a new sense of direction.
There are no pure experiences, no unmixed feelings,
no beauty that is not woven with pain.
I wanted truth.
I find several, incompatible truths.
I wanted faith.
I have met faith passionate, intense, real, and blind.
I wanted the Bible to come alive.
I find it living, breathing, and justifying violence.
Yet, like Moses, I do not come innocent to this place.
My hands are also full of blood:
the blood of my country's history –
our promising of one land to two peoples;
the blood of the holocaust
when Christian nations tried to wipe out Jews.
There is no innocence in prayer,
no innocence in religion,
no innocence in the desert –
just nowhere else to go
to avoid noticing the tenacity of evil,
or carrying my share of history, of present pain,
my share in the struggle for peace.
For, if your disciples keep silent,
these stones will cry aloud.

Janet Morley

Following in the steps of Christ

90 O Christ, as we walk through the land that you loved, in the country where you lived and taught, grant us the grace and wisdom to see clearly and understand deeply that all you had suffered was for the sake of redeeming humanity. Through your life, death, and resurrection, you have made it possible for us to have life, and have it more abundantly.

O Christ, as we follow you down the Road to Calvary
Guide us to become active participants, not curious bystanders.
O Christ, as we stand with the mourners at the Cross
Give us the love that can forgive those who trespass against us.
O Christ, as we witness the new life given to us through your Resurrection
Empower us with faith to act and spread the Good News.

Palestinian Women of Jerusalem

91 Jesus our brother,
as we dare to follow
in the steps you trod,
be our companion on the way.
May our eyes see
not only the stones that saw you
but the people who walk with you now;
may our feet tread
not only the path of your pain
but the streets of a living city;
may our prayers embrace
not only the memory of your presence
but the flesh and blood who jostle us today.
Bless us, with them, and make us long
to do justice, to love mercy,
and to walk humbly with our God. Amen

Janet Morley

Time and eternity

92 How much time is there left for me? Perhaps, after all, it is only very little. Certainly compared to the passage of a million years it would seem to be a few moments. When I consider this, it could lead me to question the whole meaning of my existence, diminishing me and making all my serious thoughts and intentions appear foolish. On the other hand time may have little value because of its length, and the few years that I have may be as important as the time it has taken to shape the continents and the seas. St Augustine asked a question we might well ask with him 'What then is time?' I know well enough what it is, provided that nobody asks me; but if I am asked what it is and try to explain, I am baffled.

While I am thinking about the future it is already arriving and making its way past me. I cannot even possess some of it for myself, for as it disappears into the past it is as far out of my reach as the future is. I may live with a calendar and a diary, as if I really did have some command over time, but it would be more true to say that time has command over me ...

How much time then is really left for **me**? How can I be in touch with something which so quickly disappears? The answer is that I only have this present moment, the moment that I am living and breathing now. In the millions of years that stream from God into creation, I am asked to be responsible for each day as it arrives. I am only given the strength and the ability to live today. The past and the future I must leave in the hands of God. He who is the Lord of all time and eternity will care for all that is out of my reach. I am simply asked to say 'Yes' to the moment as I receive it. Help me Lord to do this, to entrust the future and the past to your healing and creative love.

Community of the Resurrection

Approaching our journey's end

93 O God, who hast in thy love kept me vigorously and joyfully at work in days gone by, and dost now send me joyful and contented into silence and inactivity; grant me to find happiness in thee in all my solitary and quiet hours. In thy strength, O God, I bid farewell to all. The past thou knowest: I leave it at thy feet. Grant me grace to respond to thy divine call; to leave all that is dear on earth, and go alone to thee. Behold, I come quickly, saith the Lord. Come, Lord Jesus.

Prayer of an elderly Indian priest

94 When the signs of age begin to mark my body (and still more when they touch my mind); when the ill that is to diminish me or carry me off strikes from without or is born within me; when the painful moment comes in which I suddenly awaken to the fact that I am ill or growing old; and above all at that last moment when I feel I am losing hold of myself and am absolutely passive within the hands of the great unknown forces that have formed me; in all those dark moments, O God, grant that I may understand that it is you (provided only my faith is strong enough) who are painfully parting the fibres of my being in order to penetrate to the very marrow of my substance and bear me away within yourself.

Teilhard de Chardin SJ (1881-1955)

95 O Lord, you have made us very small, and we bring our years to an end like a tale that is told; help us to remember that beyond our brief day is the eternity of your love.

Reinhold Niebuhr (1892-1971)

Your presence

96 Grant me your Presence
In my gasping breath.
Grant me your Presence
In the hour of death.
Grant me your Presence
In my great agony.
Grant me your Presence
Through to eternity.
Grant me your Presence
At the last dark deep.
Grant me your Presence
At the final sleep.
Grant me your presence
At the long sigh.
Grant me your Presence
Till I come on high.
Grant me your Presence
When the world is past.
Grant me your Presence
When I rest at last.

In the Celtic tradition, David Adam

97 Ah! the fragrance of new grass!
I hear his footsteps coming –
The Lord of the Resurrrection!

M Jiro Sasaki, Japan

OUR DAILY LIFE – FAMILY AND COMMUNITY

ET love be genuine; hate what is evil, hold fast to what is good; love one another with mutual affection; outdo one another in showing honor ... Extend hospitality to strangers.

Romans 12. 9, 10 and 13b (New Revised Standard Version)

Something to do and think about

❖ *Gather together photographs of your family, friends, neighbours, and cuttings from the local press which reflect your links with your community. Make them a visual focus for your prayers.*

Celebrating family life

98 Lord Jesus Christ,
who was born of the house of David,
a whole family of many generations
passed down to you their traditions,
hopes and dreams,
in Bethlehem – 'the house of bread'.
In you we celebrate and affirm
the dignity of ordinary people:
a mother's obedience,
the worship of shepherds,
the perception of the wise,
the dreams and visions of the elderly Simeon and Anna ...
the meek who inherit the earth.
Your Kingdom is present in our family, village, town, or city.

Maureen Edwards

99 God is both courteous and common, awesome and ordinary,
Blessed be God!

Julian of Norwich (1342-1443)

100 For partners who love
for kids who cuddle
for grannies who listen
for friends who care:
for the stars above
for food on the table
for dogs and cats
for books and sport
we say 'thanks' to You ...
today and everyday.

Peter Millar

Deepen our loving

101 God, our Creator,
you make yourself known to us in the secret place
where we are alone in our minds,
and through our many relationships.
You make women and men in your own image,
and invite them to bear your likeness.

In motherly love you bring us to birth,
nourishing and sustaining us before we comprehend,
and so you teach us the depth and strength of love.

From the protection of fatherly love
you teach us to use the amazing gift of life,
and we learn that power is for caring.

In sisters and brothers you are beside us
in all our explorations.
In dearest friends you are our companion
through laughter and tears.

In our little ones, in sickness
and in the frailty of old age,
you claim our care
as you reveal your vulnerability.

You are there in the face of the stranger,
outcast by our indifference and rejection.

You seek us as lover, asking our answering love.
You are wounded to death at our estrangement.

These risks you take for love.

Accept our wonder.
Forgive us when we are slow to respond or understand.
Deepen our loving
that at the last
we may be at home with you.

For a wedding – Rosemary Wakelin

A blessing

102 Receive this holy fire.
Make your lives like this fire.
A holy life that is seen.
A life of God that is seen.
A life that has no end.
A life that darkness does not overcome.
May this light of God in you grow.
Light a fire that is worthy of your heads.
Light a fire that is worthy of your children.
Light a fire that is worthy of your fathers.
Light a fire that is worthy of your mothers.
Light a fire that is worthy of God.
Now go in peace.
May the Almighty protect you
today and all days.

*When people are handed the fire at the end of a ceremony they
are blessed with these words – Masai, Tanzania*

Thanksgiving for family life

103 Lord, we give thanks
for our cultural heritage,
which helps us,
through the changes of modern life,
to maintain happiness
and close family ties.

We give thanks for all that we have learnt
from our grandparents
of our traditions and folklore
and for their faith and goodness.

We give thanks
for the feeling of being loved;
for the experience of being cared for;
for the confidence in daily life
that springs from such happiness.

We give thanks
for the value of a new-born child;
for our brothers and sisters;
for the sharing of tasks;
for giving our parents love and strength,
for their wisdom
and for the benefit of their experience.

We give thanks
for your help in our daily activities:
in planting and harvesting;
for your presence in our family prayers,
and for the fellowship of those who visit us.

Young people in Kenya

Make our homes temples of worship

104 This day is dear to me above all other days for today the Beloved Lord is a guest in my house.

Kabir, North Indian mystic and poet (c 1441-1518)

105 Father, we pray thee to fill this house with thy Spirit. Here may the strong renew their strength and seek for their working lives a noble consecration. Here may the poor find succour and the friendless friendship. Here may the tempted find power, the sorrowing comfort and the bereaved find the truth that death hath no dominion over their beloved. Here let the fearing find a new courage and the doubting have their faith and hope confirmed. Here may the careless be awakened and all that are oppressed be freed. Hither may many be drawn by thy love and go hence, their doubts resolved and faith renewed, their sins forgiven and their hearts aflame with thy love. Through Jesus Christ our Lord.

From the chapel porch, Pleshey Retreat House, Chelmsford, Essex

106 Lord our God,
lead us back into the sanctuaries
where the Bible is read,
and where people listen.
Make our homes temples of worship,
and let us live
as brothers and sisters
who seek truth and compassion.

Albert Friedlander

Bless this house

107 God bless this house
from roof to floor,
and the door,
God bless us all
for evermore.
God bless the house
with fire and light;
God bless each room
with thy might;
God with thy hand
keep us right;
God be with us
in this dwelling site.

A traditional House Blessing

108 The peace of God be to you,
The peace of Christ be to you,
The peace of Spirit be to you
   To you and to your children.

Scottish traditional

109 God of love, when, in our cosiness,
we confine you within our homes,
shake our complacency.
Take us again to the stable of your incarnation
and the years of your Egyptian exile
that we may feel with you
the pain of those who are homeless and poor,
and in compassion speak out and protest
until we create a more just society
in which home and hearth are dwelling places for all.

Maureen Edwards

Evening prayer

110 Come, Lord Jesus, be our guest, stay with us, for the day is ending.
Bring to our house your poverty,
For then we shall be rich.
Bring to our house your pain,
That, sharing it, we may also share your joy.
Bring to our house your understanding of us,
That we may be freed to learn more of you.
Bring to our house all those who hurry and hirple* behind you,
That we may meet you as the Saviour of all.
With friend, with stranger,
With neighbour and the well known ones,
Be among us this night.
For the door of our house we open
And the doors of our hearts we leave ajar.

Iona Community

* 'hirple' (Scottish) – limp

Open homes

111 O God, your feast is prepared by hands like these.
Through your goodness we have this bread to offer
through your goodness we have our hands to offer
and our homes, our hearts, our hospitality.
You take our hands,
human like these hands,
skilled or clumsy, strong or aching,
smooth-skinned or knobbly or tough.
And you teach us with them
to touch with respect
the things of this earth
the hands we can reach
the hands we can't reach
invisible hands
that work for their lives
that work for our lives.
You take our homes,
everyday places
of freedom and selfishness,
of beauty and chaos and love,
and ask us to open them
not just to our friends,
our family and relations,
the neighbours we have to live with
or the people we want to impress,
but to those we don't know
and can't quite imagine –
to open our homes
and fill them with laughter
as your house is full.
You take our lives,
ordinary as wheat or cornmeal,
daily as bread,
our stumbling generosity,
our simple actions,
and you find them good enough
to open the door to your kingdom.

**Loving God, take our hands,
take our lives,
ordinary as wheat or cornmeal,
daily as bread –
our stumbling generosity,
our simple actions,
and find them good enough
to help prepare the feast
for all your people. Amen**

Janet Morley

Good neighbours

112 Almighty God, whose only begotten Son proclaimed the gospel in the villages of his childhood: hear our prayers for those who are called to live out their faith in the community of their birth and grant that they may be sustained by the peace and confidence of those who have trusted in you; through Christ our Lord. Amen

Norman Wallwork

113 Lord, help us to take good care of the paths between the houses, to use them to meet each other, for if they are not used they will become overgrown with thistles and even harder to pass. Make us communities of love, strong enough and open enough to include others. Amen

Donald Eadie

Members of one family

114   Christ of the pilgrim way,
you do not see us as rich and poor,
as educated or illiterate,
but as one family,
involved with one another,
bearing each other's burdens,
standing together.
Touch our depths with your Spirit
that we may go that extra mile
in love.

Peter Millar

115   *The Underground*

The last ones squeeze in.
The door rolls shut.
The train rumbles off.
I can't move.
I am no longer an individual, but a crowd,
A crowd that moves in one piece like jellied soup in its tin.

A nameless and indifferent crowd, probably far from you, Lord.
I am one with the crowd, and I see why it's sometimes hard
for me to rise higher.
This crowd is heavy – leaden soles on my feet, my slow feet –
a crowd too large for my overburdened skiff.
Yet, Lord, I have no right to overlook these people,
they are my brothers,
And I cannot save myself, alone.

Lord, since you wish it, I shall make for heaven in the Underground.

Michel Quoist

Growing into the Kingdom

116 O God of grace, forgive us
for building small kingdoms
within our very own lives, families,
careers, small groups,
neighbourhood and country.
Help us to realize that your Kingdom
embraces the whole earth –
the whole universe.

Jane Ella Montenegro, Philippines

117 Like the bark of a tree,
layers of influence,
weathered by experience,
encircle my life.
My roots penetrate deep into the soil,
drawing sustenance and durability
from my family,
my community's ways and traditions,
my environment,
giving me identity,
making me who I am.

Lord God, you breathe into me the life that grows,
surely and imperceptibly,
to spread branches,
strong and yet vulnerable.
Make me open to receive the water of life
and the warmth of your love,
that I may be a place
where others discover your presence and find shelter.

Maureen Edwards

Morning prayers

118 Lord, if this day you have to correct us
put us right not out of anger
but with a mother and father's love.
So may we your children
be kept free of falseness and foolishness.

Mexico

119 Heavenly Father,
we thank you for the gift of this new day,
a day, as yet, unknown to us,
untouched by us,
unlived by us.
For some, it will be spent alone,
for others, a day of anxiety and fear.
For some it will be a day to be remembered for ever
and, for many of us,
it will be a day that seems like any other day.

We pray, Lord,
that in our aloneness,
we may become more aware of your presence;
that in hours of anxiety and fear,
we may find peace of mind and spirit;
that through days of special memories,
we may grow in faith and vision;
and that in the ordinariness of daily life,
we may catch a glimpse of your love to sustain us,
this day and for evermore. Amen

Brenda Armstrong

Home improvements

120 You can't trust anyone these days.
Take this Jesus.
Seemed OK.
We asked him in
(just being neighbourly –
you know how it is).

Over dinner he was polite enough
apart from a habit of continually
turning the small talk into conversation.
He was even keen to hear about
our plans for home improvements.
So we showed him round.

This was the big mistake.
When it came down to it
he wasn't interested
in the kitchen units
or the bathroom tiles
or the artificial ceiling in the lounge,
but kept peering into cupboards uninvited
(as if we had dry rot)
and prizing up the edges of the carpet
(as if we had woodworm)

and finally he disappeared into the cellar
(heaven knows what he found down there)
emerging with a hammer
and a pick axe
and a drill
and a pocketful of drawings
and, smiling in a most alarming way, said
I've just had a much better idea

and started smashing down the walls.

G Rust

OUR DAILY LIFE –
WORK AND LEISURE

HEN you pray, say this:
'Father:
May your holy name be honoured;
may your Kingdom come.
Give us day by day the food we need.
Forgive us our sins,
for we forgive everyone who does us wrong.
And do not bring us to hard testing.'

Luke 11.2-4 (Good News Bible)

Something to do and think about

❖ *Create a worship corner or table in your room. Place on it a cross, and/or other meaningful objects. Include symbols of*

> *your work, or the work you used to do if you are retired or unemployed,*

> *ways in which you serve the community,*

> *your home life,*

> *your leisure activities.*

It's hard to be a carpenter

121 I wonder what He charged for chairs
At Nazareth.
And did men try to beat Him down,
And boast about it in the town,
'I bought it cheap for half a crown
From that mad carpenter'?
And did they promise and not pay,
Put it off to another day,
O did they break His heart that way,
My Lord the Carpenter?
I wonder did He have bad debts,
And did He know my fears and frets?
The Gospel writer here forgets
To tell about the Carpenter.
But that's just what I want to know.
Ah! Christ in glory, here below
Men cheat and lie to one another so
It's hard to be a carpenter.

G A Studdert Kennedy

122 Almighty God, who didst ordain that thy Son, Jesus Christ, should
labour with his hands to supply his own needs, and the needs of
others: Teach us we pray thee, that no labour is mean, and all labour
is divine, to which thou dost call us; to the glory of thy holy Name.

Eric Milner-White and G W Briggs

123 Lord, let me not live to be useless.

John Wesley

Serving the community

124 Let us pray for those whose daily work gives them power over other people:
> For those concerned in government;
> For those in charge of companies;
> For the leaders of trades unions;
> For those whose work influences how we think;
> For ...

Lord, we pray that they may not shirk those responsibilities that go with their power, and may serve not only their own interests but those of others, with wisdom, honesty, fairness and kindness.
Lord you have work for each one of us:
Teach us to serve you in all we do.

Let us pray for those who work for the public services in our society:
> For those who look after our health;
> For those who look after our safety;
> For those who teach and train;
> For those who give us advice and support;
> For those who provide the essentials for life;
> For ...

Lord, we pray that these people may find satisfaction and joy in their work, and may serve those they seek to help with patience, courage and understanding.
Lord, you have work for each one of us:
Teach us to serve you in all we do.

Let us pray for those whose work is not rewarded by a wage:
> For voluntary workers in areas of need;
> For housewives and parents;
> For those who raise funds for charities;
> For those who serve as community leaders;
> For ...

Lord, we pray that society may value these people and give them the support that they need. We pray that they may fulfil their duties with humility and generosity of spirit.
Lord, you have work for each one of us:
Teach us to serve you in all we do.

Let us pray for those who are finding their work difficult:
> For those whose jobs are repetitive and dull;
> For those who cannot get along with their fellow workers;
> For those who have been put in a moral dilemma;
> For those who cannot cope with the demands of their work;
> For ...

Lord, we pray for those who dread the working day and we ask that you will grant them the courage they need, whether to persevere as they are, or to change their lives.
Lord, you have work for each one of us:
Teach us to serve you in all we do.   *Christine Odell*

Blessed in the common tasks

125 We ask you to bless those for whom life is very ordinary:
Those who feel that nothing ever happens;
Those who feel that life is dull and uninteresting;
Those who are bored and fed up with the routine of everyday.
Teach all such that it is in the common tasks they
find or miss their destiny and their reward.
You know us better than we know ourselves. Bless us, not as we ask,
but as you in your wisdom know that we need.

William Barclay

You asked for my hands

126 You asked for my hands
that you might use them for your purpose.
I gave them for a moment then withdrew them
for the work was hard.

You asked for my mouth
to speak out against injustice.
I gave you a whisper that I might not be accused.

You asked for my eyes
to see the pain of poverty.
I closed them for I did not want to see.

You asked for my life
that you might work through me.
I gave a small part that I might not get too involved.

Lord, forgive my calculated efforts to serve you,
only when it is convenient for me to do so,
only in those places where it is safe to do so,
and only with those who make it easy to do so.

Father, forgive me,
renew me
send me out
as a usable instrument
that I might take seriously
the meaning of your cross.

Joe Seremane, South Africa

I give my hands to you Lord

127 I give my hands to you Lord
I give my hands to you

I offer the work I do Lord
I offer the work I do

I give my thoughts to you Lord
I give my thoughts to you

I give my plans to you Lord
I give my plans to you

Give your hands to me Lord
Give your hands to me

Let your love set me free Lord
Let your love set me free

Keep me close to you Lord
Keep me close to you.

David Adam in the Celtic tradition

128 Lord, give me love and commonsense,
And standards that are high;
Give me calm and confidence,
And please, a twinkle in my eye!

The Christian Worker's Prayer

For lives of integrity

129 Most merciful Father, we commend to your care and protection those whose work is dangerous, and especially those who risk their lives for the lives of others.
We thank you for their courage and their devotion to duty; and we pray that in every hour of need they may know that you are with them and may fear no evil ...

Frank Colquhoun

130 Almighty and everlasting God, we pray for those engaged in the industrial life of our nation.
   Remove bitterness, distrust and prejudice between employers and employees.
   Give to all a spirit of tolerance, and an earnest desire to seek for justice and equity, that they may work together for the common good; through Jesus Christ our Lord.

W A Hampton

131 God of wholeness,
you have created us bodily,
that our work and faith may be one.
May we offer our worship
from lives of integrity;
and maintain the fabric of this world
with hearts that are set on you,
through Jesus Christ, Amen.

(Ecclesiasticus / Ben Sirach 38.24 – end)
Janet Morley

That we may not be ashamed

132 We thank thee, God, for the moments of fulfilment:
  the end of a day's work,
  the harvest of sugar cane,
  the birth of a child,
for in these pauses, we feel the rhythm of the eternal. Amen

Hawaii

133 Lord God, who sees into the hearts of all,
remind us that we have no secrets from you.
Give us courage to be honest in all our dealings,
to short-change no-one, to pay our taxes gladly.
For you, O Lord, are the God of truth and justice,
and we wish to be like you.

Sheila Cassidy

134 Grant us grace, our Father, to do our work this day as workmen who
need not be ashamed. Give us the spirit of diligence and honest
enquiry in our quest for truth, the spirit of charity in all our dealings
with our fellows, and the spirit of gaiety, courage, and a quiet mind
in facing all tasks and responsibilities.

Reinhold Niebuhr (1892-1971)

135 The love and affection of heaven be to you,
The love and affection of the saints be to you,
The love and affection of the angels be to you,
The love and affection of the sun be to you,
The love and affection of the moon be to you,
  Each day and night of your lives,
  To keep you from haters, to keep you from harmers,
   to keep you from oppressors.

Scottish traditional

God's blessing be yours

136 O God, who hast bound us together in this bundle of life, give us grace to understand how our lives depend upon the courage, the industry, the honesty, and the integrity of our fellow-men; that we may be mindful of their needs, grateful for their faithfulness, and faithful in our responsibilities to them; through Jesus Christ our Lord.

Reinhold Niebuhr (1892-1971)

137 May there always be work for your hands to do
May your purse always hold a coin or two
May the sun always shine on your window pane
May a rainbow be certain to follow each rain
May the hand of a friend always be near you
May God fill your heart with gladness to cheer you.

An Irish Blessing

138 God's blessing be yours,
And well may it befall you;
Christ's blessing be yours,
And well be you entreated;
The Spirit's blessing be yours,
And well spend you your lives,
Each day that you rise up,
Each night that you lie down.

Scottish traditional

Unemployed

139 Creator God,
I've got this idea I must be active and busy,
doing big things in your name:
prophesying to the world,
eradicating poverty.
Yet it is the everyday struggles
which are so demanding:
just about making ends meet,
maintaining some dignity.
I might not have been the greatest worker
but now I've been put on the scrap heap.

Teacher Christ
We need to learn a new way of being.
Show us how to be prophets in every situation,
employed or unemployed,
underpaid or overworked,
so that the justice of labour shared
may truly build up your body
in honour and rejoicing.

Janet Lees

140 *In the autumn of 1992 the British Government announced the closure of 30 coal mines. The names of the 30 pits were read out as a roll call.*

God, you call us from the dark womb
to seek and grasp abundant living
for all the world;
Give us energy and wisdom
to mine all possibilities of life
today and tomorrow.

Alison Norris

Looking at the future

141 Lord, when I think about the future,
I begin to worry ...
The future stretches out before me
like a long dark tunnel,
leading into the unknown.
After my exams,
will I get to university?
Or will I begin the endless search for a job?
Will I make enough money?

Lord, my future is in your hands.
Help me to look honestly
at my own ability
and to know if I have the right skills
for the jobs that attract me ...
Help me to choose a career
in which I can work honestly,
and avoid corruption and immorality ...

Lord, I would like to be independent
and never have to rely
on the charity of others.
But help me to face the possibility
of unemployment if that is my future.
If I fail, give me courage to begin again ...

From a prayer by Kenyan young people

142 Father, there are those among us who, like Simeon, have worked and taught and showed us something of your Kingdom. Keep them fresh in their faith, and a continued inspiration to the young among us. Make us sensitive to their growing physical needs and give us a generous spirit in serving them.

Prayer from Pakistan for elderly pastors and church workers

Our need of space

143 About this time I always feel that I shall never get through everything that I have to do. There are always people to see, letters to write, plans to be made, and then there is all the moving about. As fast as a space begins to appear it is immediately filled up with something else which is important.

Yes Lord, it does all appear to be important and necessary. I cannot let people down, leave letters unanswered, make no plans. In one sense I feel committed to do all these things that come to me. I try to believe that they come to me from you ...

But why is it that there seems to be no time just to be quiet; time to be still, with you. In my heart I want to have time to pray, but there always seems to be something else to be done. Whenever I make a resolution about it, it is broken as soon as I begin.

Sometimes I wonder if only **some** of the work is absolutely necessary, and comes from you, and whether the rest of it I have taken on just to prove that I am occupied in important business. Perhaps I say 'yes' sometimes when I could say 'no', and I do not allow the space and time to exist.

In the end Lord – it is not so much what I do, as what kind of person I am who is doing it. If I could give more time to being still and talking to you, then perhaps I would do things with more love and less of the rush and clatter.

Help me Lord to give you time: to leave space in my day for quiet and prayer. Help me to put you first in my life, and after that the work that you have given me to do.

Community of the Resurrection

Our leisure time

144 Lord, you have created us so that we need regular periods of rest. The work of the day must be followed by the sleep of the night. A day off each week is precious and necessary to us. After long stretches of work we need holidays. We believe that these conditions of our life are an expression of your will. For Jesus recognized our need for rest; and one way people have thought of life after death is as the everlasting rest of your people.

And yet we know that relaxation is not just a matter of stopping work. Some of us quickly become bored when we are not working. Or work has left some of us so exhausted that we cannot enjoy our leisure. Or other people make heavy demands on our spare time. It seems selfish to insist on time to ourselves, but we cannot be ourselves without it. We do not want to consume our time and energy on trifles, and yet if we cannot sometimes forget all about ideals and need and service we find we have not been refreshed after all.

Father, guide us in this as in other things. Help us to relax as we should, knowing that the world is in your hands, not in ours. And take up our leisure time into your purpose, so that when we begin our work again we do so the better for having rested.

Caryl Micklem

145 The red sun dips into the shining sea
And marks the ending of the winter days;
Along the land the calm of evening steals,
While all my heart is lifted up in praise.

Nagata, a Japanese leprosy patient

Morning and evening

146 Eternal God
We say good morning to you.
Hallowed be your name.
Early in the morning, before we begin our work,
we praise your glory.
Renew our bodies as fresh as the morning flowers.
Open our inner eyes, as the sun casts new light
upon the darkness
which prevailed over the night.
Deliver us from all captivity.
Give us wings of freedom,
as a mighty stream running continuously
from day to day.
We thank you for the gift of this morning,
and a new day to work with you. Amen

Masao Takenaka, Japan

147 Lord, I thank Thee for night,
the time of cool and quiet,
the time of sweet enchantment
when a deep mystery pervades everything.
The time when soul speaks to soul in common desire
to partake of the hush of the ineffable.
The time when the moon and the stars
speak to people of their high calling and destiny.
The time of repose and calm
when the fever of the mind subsides
and uncertainty gives place
to the sense of eternal purpose.
O Lord, I thank Thee for night.

Chandran Devanesen, India (adapted)

OUR DAILY LIFE – BROKENNESS AND GRIEF

 CRY aloud to the Lord;
to the Lord I plead aloud for mercy.
I pour out my complaint before him
and unfold my troubles in his presence.
When my spirit is faint within me,
you are there to watch over my steps.

I cry to you, Lord,
and say, 'You are my refuge ...'

Psalm 142.1-3, 5a (Revised English Bible)

Of the Aberfan tragedy:

God is not a God who, from the top of the mountain caused or permitted it to happen, but a God who received at the foot of the mountain its appalling impact.

W H Vanstone, Love's Endeavour, Love's Expense (DLT)

Something to do and think about

❖ *Add a candle to your worship table. Light it and reflect on the warmth of the flame, its continuous movement, flickering, changing shape and colour, brightness ...*

❖ *If there are flowers or plants in your room, reflect on their fragility, colour, shape, perfume, transparency, life ...*

❖ *Or look out of the window and reflect on what you see. If you live in a built-up area, where do you see signs of hope?*

Let me forget my sorrow

148 Lord, I am angry because I am so poor
and a few others have too much.
Let me forget my anger and remember
you will give me bread daily.

Lord, I am sad and tired; my children
ask too much of me.
Let me forget my sorrow in knowing
you are always there.

Lord, I get impatient because
my friends are too busy to listen.

Let me come to you because
you always listen and are never
too busy to hear my prayer,
and grant me a little peace
for me to spread around and share.

Pat Young

149 O wild and terrible God,
mysterious, powerful, beyond all knowing,
we marvel at your gentle patience,
at the unbelievable tenderness of your love.
Draw us, weary and limping from our struggle,
back into the safety of your embrace.

Sheila Cassidy

God is with us

150 Rise up, you poor,
You know your own need of God
Your hearts are free from the dazzle and
enslavement that wealth and property bring.

Rise up and see the presence of God in your midst,
affirming you and working among you and through you.

Rise up, you whose hearts are breaking.
Your mourning and cries to heaven are being heard.
Raise your crying louder so that the whole earth
will hear your cry.

Rise up, do not keep your grief quiet
And your mourning will pierce the hearts
of the stony hearted
And you shall be comforted in your grief.

Based on Matthew 5.3-10 David McManus, Hope Community

151 Lord our God, we pray for those who are defeated
by pain, sorrow, despair or loneliness.
May they know the victory of love,
the song of hope and a glimpse of glory.

Bernard Thorogood

The Comrade God

152 Thou who dost dwell in depths of timeless being,
Watching the years as moments passing by,
Seeing the things that lie beyond our seeing,
Constant, unchanged, as aeons dawn and die;

Thou who canst count the stars upon their courses,
Holding them all in the hollow of Thy hand,
Lord of the world with its myriad of forces
Seeing the hills as single grains of sand;

Art Thou so great that this our bitter crying
Sounds in Thine ears like sorrow of a child?
Hast Thou looked down on centuries of sighing,
And, like a heartless mother, only smiled?
Since in Thy sight to-day is as to-morrow,
And while we strive Thy victory is won,
Hast Thou no tears to shed upon our sorrow?
Art Thou a staring splendour like the sun?

Dost Thou not heed the helpless sparrow's falling?
Canst Thou not see the tears that women weep?
Canst Thou not hear Thy little children calling?
Dost Thou not watch above them as they sleep?

Then, O My God, Thou art too great to love me,
Since Thou dost reign beyond the reach of tears,
Calm and serene the cruel stars above me,
High and remote from human hopes and fears.

Only in Him can I find home to hide me,
Who on the Cross was slain to rise again;
Only with Him, my Comrade God, beside me,
Can I go forth to war with sin and pain.

G A Studdert Kennedy

The disturbing face of God

153 The man sitting in the doorway,
dirty blanket wrapped around the hunched shoulders.
A carrier bag containing all his worldly goods.
'Spare some change?'
Do I see your face in his, Lord
or an eyesore to be tidied up
and put out of my sight?

The women standing at the street corner
eyeing up likely clients,
waiting for a car to pull up
or the muttered word of the man walking past.
Do I see your face in theirs, Lord
or only exploiters of sexuality to be despised
and put out of my sight?

The young man sitting in the car
while a succession of children and youths
come to exchange the proceeds of petty crime
for the dangerous excitement of pills and powder.
Do I see your face in his, Lord
or a deadly exploiter of human weakness
to be given the worst of punishments
and put out of my sight?

Crowds push past along the street,
men and women, carrying their bags and brief cases,
all burdened with the luggage of life,
of missed opportunities, broken relationships and lost dreams.
Do I see your face in theirs, Lord
or only an anonymous mass of people to be ignored
and put out of my sight?

If I see your face in theirs, Lord
I can't put them out of my sight
whatever their problems or failings;
however evil their actions or how many they are.
Even when it's painful and disturbing, Lord
help me always to see your face in others.

Simon Oxley

Downward mobility

154 *Reflect – and pray that you may follow the way of Jesus:*

The poor and the weak have revealed to me
the great secret of Jesus.
If you wish to follow him
you must not try to climb the ladder of success and power,
becoming more and more important.
Instead, you must walk *down* the ladder,
to meet and walk with people
who are broken and in pain.
The light is there, shining in the darkness,
the darkness of their poverty.
The poor with whom you are called to share your life
are the sick and the old;
people out of work,
young people caught up in the world of drugs,
people angry because they were terribly hurt
when they were young,
people with disabilities or sick with Aids,
or just out of prison ...
people who are oppressed
because of the colour of their skin ...
people in pain.

Jean Vanier

For those who suffer

155 Let us pray
for those who suffer
because they love:
for the bereaved
and those who are anxious
about relatives or friends,
for those who weep
at the evils of the world,
for those who deny themselves
to give loving care.
(For ...)

In the name of Christ,
who gave himself on the Cross
in obedience to love,
Lord, in your mercy:
Hear our prayer.

Let us pray
for those who suffer
because of their own actions:
those who suffer guilt,
whose lives are full of regret,
those who despise
the people they are,
those who have made themselves
unloving or unlovable.
(For ...)

In the name of Christ,
who pronounced the forgiveness of sins,
Lord, in your mercy:
Hear our prayer.

Lord, on the Cross of Christ we see you sharing in the suffering of
your world. We rejoice to know that in our darkest hours you are with
us, and we commend into your love those whom we know who are
suffering in any way. Amen

Christine Odell

For all who despair

156 In me there is darkness,
But with you there is light;
I am lonely, but you do not leave me;
I am feeble in heart, but with you there is help;
I am restless, but with you there is peace.
In me there is bitterness, but with you there is patience;
I do not understand your ways,
But you know the way for me.

Dietrich Bonhoeffer

157 Father,
we pray for those
who know the suffering
of total despair:
for the terminally ill
and the grief-stricken;
for the depressed
and for those consumed by guilt;
for those who have lost their faith
in life, in others, in you.
We bring before you
those who feel totally alone
when faced with fears and pain
that threaten to overwhelm them.

Christine Odell

Open our lives to your healing

158 Lord you are a present help in trouble.
Come revive
Redeem
Restore
In our darkness come as light
In our sadness come as joy
In our troubles come as peace
In our weakness come as strength
Come Lord to our aid
Revive
Redeem
Restore us

O Lord
   Open our eyes to your Presence
   Open our minds to your grace
   Open our lips to your praises
   Open our hearts to your love
   Open our lives to your healing
   And be found among us.

In the Celtic tradition, David Adams

159 O God, grant that I may do and suffer all things this day for the glory of thy name.

Used by the Cure d'Ars (1786-1859)

Released from pain

160 Lord Jesus Christ,
who shed tears at the death of a friend,
you were with me in the long vigil
as my loved one lost consciousness,
slowly dying.
You were present in the reassuring words
and practical caring of those who tended her,
in the thoughts and prayers of many friends,
and in the strength and support of family and community,
reminding me of roots and solidarity
not so clearly recognized before.
You showed me that she was no longer imprisoned
in a fragile, ageing body,
tossed between experiences of joy and pain,
but free, re-born in all the innocence of a child,
bathed in your glory,
clothed in your goodness,
secure at last in your presence,
to weep no more,
but – transformed –
to enjoy the reality of your love
which never ends.

Maureen Edwards

161 O God who brought us to birth,
and in whose arms we die:
we entrust to your embrace
our beloved *sister*.
Give *her* release from *her* pain,
courage to meet the darkness,
and grace to let go into new life,
through Jesus Christ, Amen.

Janet Morley

To live again with joy

162 I don't believe in death
Who mocks in silent stealth;
He robs us only of a breath,
Not of a lifetime's wealth.

I don't believe the tomb
Imprisons us in the earth,
It's but another loving womb
Preparing our new birth.

I do believe in Life
Empowered from above,
Till, freed from stress and worldly strife
We soar through realms above.

I do believe that then,
In joy that never ends,
We'll meet all those we've loved, again,
And celebrate our friends!

Pauline Webb

163 Death is not extinguishing the light
but putting out the lamp
because the dawn has come.

Rabindranath Tagore

Hope springs eternal

164 The wheel of the law turns without pause.

After rain, good weather
in the wink of an eye.

The universe throws off its muddy clothes.

For ten thousand miles
the landscape
spreads out like a beautiful brocade
light breezes, smiling flowers.

High in the trees, amongst
the sparkling leaves
all the birds sing at once.
Man and animals rise up reborn.

What could be more natural?
After sorrow, comes happiness.

Vietnam

165 May the eye of the great God,
The eye of the God of glory,
The eye of the Virgin's Son,
The eye of the gentle Spirit
Aid you and shepherd you
    In every time,
Pour upon you every hour
    Mildly and generously.

Scottish traditional

OUR DAILY LIFE – CHURCH AND COMMUNITY

 Y friends, think what sort of people you are, whom God has called. Few of you are wise by any human standard, few powerful or of noble birth. Yet, to shame the wise, God has chosen what the world counts folly, and to shame what is strong, God has chosen what the world counts weakness. He has chosen things without rank or standing in the world, mere nothings, to overthrow the existing order.

1 Corinthians 1.26-28 (Revised English Bible)

Something to do and think about

❖ *On a small card, describe your vision for your local church and community. Keep it in this book, or in your Bible, or place it on your worship table, as a reminder.*

❖ *Write a prayer that begins with your vision.*

As your family, Lord ...

166 Father God,
Joyfully, we come into your presence,
Obediently, we worship and adore you,
Penitently, we acknowledge our failures,
Gratefully, we receive your forgiveness,
Pleadingly, we intercede for others,
Hopefully, we go out into all the world. Amen

Brenda Armstrong

167 We praise and thank you, Lord,
for the world you have created
and the precious gift of life you have given to each of us.
Because of the pressures of daily life,
we take everything for granted
and don't always take time to look around
and appreciate your great work.

We praise and thank you for the church family,
for relationships and friendships formed;
for the fellowship and love we receive in your name.

We praise and thank you for our families and friends,
for without their love and encouragement
we would find it hard to cope with everyday life.

We praise and thank you for the greatest gift of all,
your own Son, Jesus Christ,
who died on the cross, in obedience to you,
for every one of us. Amen.

Margaret Sedgeman

Bind us together

168 God, your church is where ordinary people gather
with all their varying needs –
 women and men,
 young and old,
 simple and capable,
 sinners and saints,
 poor and rich.
Hear us, heal us and bind us together, O Lord.

The church is where your gospel is proclaimed
and your truths discussed, week by week
 in word and sacraments,
 in mid-week fellowships,
 in dialogue and debate.
We pray for all who preach and lead us in worship,
and for ourselves in our daily witness to Christ.
Hear us, heal us and bind us together, O Lord.

Many come seeking refreshment and renewal:
 some are overworked, others are unemployed;
 some are lonely, bereaved or sad;
 some are successful, others are disappointed;
 some have illness, stresses, or anxieties about others.
Hear us, heal us and bind us together, O Lord.

Through your church we find newness of life,
 light, joy and laughter,
 and all the richness and variety of your gifts to us.
 Help us to use your gifts more creatively.
Hear us, heal us and bind us together, O Lord.

Audrey Stanley

The building of Christ

169 Thank God for struggling churches
Struggling to mend broken windows
   and clear up after the break-in.
Struggling to pay their way
   in spite of diminishing resources.
Struggling to remain involved with the rest of the Church
   in spite of fewer people to represent them.
Struggling to care for the local community
   in spite of indifference or hostility.
Struggling to keep their confidence
   when hearing the 'success stories' of other Christians.

Thank God for struggling churches:
   reminding us of the cost of being faithful,
   shining as a light in the darkness
   and a sign of hope for us all.

Simon Oxley

170 O GRACIOUS God and most merciful Father, who hast vouchsafed us
the rich and precious jewel of thy holy word: Assist us with thy Spirit
that it may be written in our hearts to our everlasting comfort, to
reform us, to renew us according to thine own image, to build us up
and edify us into the perfect building of thy Christ, sanctifying and
increasing in us all heavenly virtues. Grant this, O heavenly Father,
for the same Jesus Christ's sake.

Preface to the Geneva Bible. Sometimes attributed to
King Edward VI (1537-53)

We confess

171 We confess that when we come to worship you
we are more concerned about what worship offers us.
We praise you on Sunday
but forget you in the busyness of Monday.
We have diaries full of church activities
but do not spend time on our relationships with each other
and with you.
We make our offering
but do not feel accountable to you for the rest of our money.

We confess that we pray for a long list of people
but do not make personal contact with them to show we care.
We read the Bible to feed our faith
but do not let your word challenge the way we live in the world.
We help with the Christian Aid Week collection
but do not work for justice for the poor of the world.

Forgive us and help us to build on the good we do
so that our living may become more whole.

Simon Oxley

172 Living God, disturber and saviour of your people,
open our eyes to the truth of your Word,
the state of our lives
and the condition of our nation,
that with faith and hope
we may pray:
your kingdom come,
your will be done on earth as in heaven.

Brian Haymes

Our lack of vision

173 O God, key of life,
where our churches lie locked and empty
open us to the possibility of serving you
through serving our community.
Forgive us our lack of vision.

O Christ, head of the body,
where we lock up the body's treasures
release us to new ways of service,
through the offering of each member's gift.
Forgive us our lack of courage.

O Spirit of God, revealer of truth,
where we fail to recognize you,
create in us an awareness of your presence
in and through the joy and hurt of life.
Forgive us our lack of commitment.

In the forgiving power of the Spirit,
may we rebuild this household of faith
to be Christ's body in the world
and find new life
in an open community
of God's purpose
in this place.

Kate McIlhagga

Willingness to change

174 Lord, take the shoes off this Church
not only physically, outwardly, actually,
   but inwardly also.
Lord, take the shoes off this Church –
the shoes of pride and of fear,
   complacency and factionalism.
Lord, take the shoes off this Church
that the quality of its worship may touch
   the whole life of this people:
And to this end, put the shoes on this
   Church that it may
go out to serve all men and women everywhere
   Lord.

Church Missionary Society

175 Lord send us apostles to increase our faith;
send us prophets to open our eyes;
send us teachers to instruct our hearts;
send us evangelists to lead us to Christ;
send us pastors to bind us in love
and send us healers to make us whole;
through Christ our Lord. Amen

Norman Wallwork

176 O God, help us not to despise or oppose what we do not
understand.

William Penn (1644-1718)

For the local church community

177 Father, Son and Holy Spirit,
One God, in perfect Community,
Look now on us ...
And hear our prayer for our community:
Where there is falseness ...
Smother it by your truth;
Where there is coldness ...
Kindle the flame of your love;
Where there is joy and hope ...
Free us to share it together;
Where there is anything
We will not do for ourselves ...
Make us discontent until it is done.
And make us one ...
As you are one.

Before God and you who are near me,
I release anything I hold against you.
I regret all I have done to harm you.
I stand beside the wrong in my life
And ask God's forgiveness.

Before God and you who are near us,
We release anything we hold against you.
We regret all we have done to harm you.
We stand beside the wrong in our lives
And ask God's forgiveness. *(Silence)*

The Lord Jesus Christ says to us, each one:
'Go and sin no more,
Come and follow me.'
Now bind our hands with honesty
As we offer them to each other
And our prayer to you :
(The Lord's prayer, joining hands if appropriate).

Iona Community

Praying together for the community

178 In sharing our anxieties and our love, our poverty and our prosperity, we partake of your divine presence.

Canaan Banana, first President of Zimbabwe

179 We pray for all who are depressed, feeling that they have no one to turn to.
We pray for all your children of ... *(the name of your community).*
We thank you for them.
We pray for all the people who once belonged to our churches, who no longer go anywhere, who are disappointed, disillusioned or lonely.
We pray for all those who are old, who over the years have forgotten how to pray, have lost their faith and now feel they are not worthy to come to church or to be loved.
Unite our communities, so that they can voice their lives and their fears for justice to the people in power.
We pray the Churches will speak out and reach out still further into the community to touch people's lives with God's love. May we forget tradition and work together as one to teach people about the precious gift of our Lord Jesus Christ.

From an ecumenical workshop on the estates of Hartcliffe and Withywood, Bristol

180 O Lord, you have promised
that your disciples are to catch men and women.
Grant that our nets may be cast
as widely and as deeply as your own great love.

John Carden

Christ on our doorstep

181 Lord Jesus Christ,
you stand at the door and knock,
but we open the door,
cautiously and reluctantly,
afraid you might come right in,
making difficult demands,
as you do of those who have many gifts:
demands of accessibility,
time and hospitality,
as you come
in the elderly,
the disabled,
the bereaved,
the unemployed,
young people,
little children,
people different from ourselves ...
our neighbours!

Lord, we have too much ...
too many possessions
blocking the entrance hall for you to come in!
Our material concerns and anxieties
hide the richer gifts you have given
for service to the community
and fellowship within your body.

'Happy are the poor,
happy are the hungry ...'
Only emptiness compels and enables us
to open the door
to begin to receive you
through those who know their need.

Maureen Edwards

Use us, Lord

182 O God, holy and righteous,
greater than human thoughts can imagine or tongues express,
source of all love, and love itself,
you have revealed your nature through Jesus Christ
and so we praise you.
This love fills us your people,
enabling us to live and work for your Kingdom.
Use us, Lord, as channels of your grace.

Heavenly Father, we speak so many words;
it is easy to talk about the weather,
our families, our interests, our aches and pains!
Forgive us for remaining silent over the deeper things:
our thoughts and feelings, our blessings and faith.
Make us more sensitive to the needs of others,
and bold to speak the words they need to hear from you.
Use us, Lord, as channels of your grace.

We thank you, Lord, for fellowship around your table,
for here we acknowledge that we are one body.
Holding out our hands to receive the bread,
mysteriously we receive your very self,
given in self-emptying love.
May the Bread of Life so nourish and strengthen us
that we may help to alleviate the physical or spiritual hunger
of neighbours you have given us.
Use us, Lord, as channels of your grace.

We praise you, Lord God,
that in love you send your Spirit to enable and empower us.
Help us to live in the reality
of the promise of the Spirit's continuing presence with us,
praising you for every sign of peace, justice and reconciliation
that we encounter.
Use us, Lord, as channels of your grace.

Lord God, we thank you that much is being done in your name
to lessen suffering in our world.
You are always calling us to leave self behind,
to follow Christ, to be used by you
to answer the prayers and needs of others.
Help us to use the faith we have found
to reshape the world around us.
Use us, Lord, as channels of your grace.

Spirit of God, without you we can do nothing.
Only as we are filled with your love can we reach out to others.
We pray that you will move, live and grow in us
until our ways are your ways
so that our small hearts no longer limit
the greatness of your resources,
and others begin to see you 'living' and 'working in our world'.
Use us, Lord, as channels of your grace

Based on the hymn 'There's a spirit in the air' by Brian Wren
Ruth Richards

I am no longer my own, but yours

183 I am no longer my own, but yours. Put me to what you will, rank me with whom you will; put me to doing, put me to suffering; let me be employed for you or laid aside for you, exalted for you or brought low for you; let me be full, let me be empty; let me have all things, let me have nothing; I freely and wholeheartedly yield all things to your pleasure and disposal. And now, glorious and blessed God, Father, Son, and Holy Spirit, you are mine and I am yours. So be it. And the covenant now made on earth, let it be ratified in heaven. Amen

The Methodist Covenant Service

Called to love and reconciliation

184 Eternal God, fill your Church with the Holy Spirit;
that, as in the days of Pentecost,
we may be set afire to share
with power and conviction
the gospel of salvation.

Kindle your sacred flame
on the altars of our hearts,
that we may show to the whole world,
that you are truly a forgiving, saving and loving God.

**Lord, uphold us by your power
and teach us how to demonstrate your love in our lives**

Help us to identify with the needs of broken parts of our society,
and become the reconciling presence of your Son
within that brokenness.

**Lord, uphold us by your power
and teach us how to demonstrate your love in our lives**

Give us faith to meet the challenges
and opportunities of the present
and press forward into the future with hope and confidence.

Lord, teach us how to make the leap of faith into the unknown,
pouring ourselves out in love for others,
crossing boundaries to identify with the struggles,
suffering and needs of others;
for your sake. Amen

Lesley Anderson, Panama

Humour and holiness!

185 When we are tempted in our pride
To dizzy heights of sin,
Beneath our feet, O Lord, provide
A ripe banana skin,
And when we yearn at someone's head
To let a brickbat fly,
Give us the grace to use instead
A well-aimed custard pie.

When cherished institutions stand
Before your Throne of Grace,
With good intentions in each hand,
And egg on every face,
Teach us to query grand designs
With laughter born of tears,
For deep in earth's jam-butty mines
Your rainbow still appears.

Along with zeal to do your will
We ask a sense of fun,
A touch of sugar on the pill,
A currant in the bun.
Like him who saw a desert bush
With heaven's glory crowned,
May we, through the incongruous,
Discover holy ground.

Elizabeth Cosnett

ONE WORLD – CROSSING BARRIERS

 HERE is no such thing as Jew and Greek, slave and freeman, male and female; for you are all one person in Christ Jesus.

Galatians 3.28 (Revised English Bible)

Something to do and think about

❖ *Get to know someone of another culture in your community, and learn from his or her experience.*

We confess

186 Lord God, you set us over the world you created,
but we confess that we have made its rich resources our gods.
We do not want to recognize
that the powerless and those who have nothing
are first in your Kingdom.
We want power and yet we are weak:
we remain silent spectators,
afraid of the consequences of speaking out against evil.
Lord have mercy.
Forgive us and change us.

Lord Jesus Christ, you love the world and its people
and showed us how to serve one another in partnership.
You challenged old and narrow forms of thought
and broke down the walls of hostility
that separate us from one another –
in the family,
the community and the world.
We confess our obstinacy in setting up new barriers;
our failure to accept one another as equals;
our unwillingness to change
and reach out in love and service to others.
Lord have mercy.
Forgive us and change us.

Holy Spirit, in your power we are called to go out
into our neighbourhood and all the world
to share the good news of the Kingdom among us.
You lead us into new situations
and challenge us with new ideas and ways to change the world.
We confess that more often we seek strength and comfort
from your indwelling for our immediate needs
and resist the new ways and truths you lead us to consider.
Lord, have mercy.
Forgive us and change us.

Maureen Edwards

Encounter Christ

187 You broke down the barriers,
When you crept in beside us
For in Jesus – the smiling Jesus
   the story-telling Jesus
   the controversial Jesus
   the annoying Jesus
   the loving and forgiving Jesus
Your hands touched all,
And touched us,
showing how in Christ there is neither Jew nor Gentile,
neither male nor female:
All are one in Jesus Christ and for this we praise you

You opened our eyes
To see how the hands of the rich were empty
And the hearts of the poor were full.
You dared to take the widow's mite,
   the child's loaves,
   the babe at the breast,
And in these simple things
To point out the path to your Kingdom.
You said, 'Follow me',
For on our own we could never discover
That in Christ there is neither Jew nor Gentile,
neither male nor female:
All are one in Jesus Christ and for this we praise you

You gave us hands to hold:
Black hands and white hands,
African hands and Asian hands,
The clasping hands of lovers,
And the reluctant hands of those
Who don't believe they are worth holding.
And when we wanted to shake our fist,
You still wanted to hold our hand,
because in Christ there is neither Jew nor Gentile,
neither male nor female:
All are one in Jesus Christ and for this we praise you

Here in the company of the neighbour whom we know
   and the stranger in our midst,
   and the self from whom we turn,
We ask to love as Jesus loved.
Make this the place and the time, good Lord,
When heaven and earth merge into one,
And we in word and flesh can grasp
That there is neither Jew nor Gentile,
neither male nor female:
All are one in Jesus Christ and for this we praise you. Amen

Prayer used during a conference at the Department of Mission,
Selly Oak Colleges, 1992

Forgive our narrow vision

188 Lord, we thank you for our world –
for its infinite varieties of people, colours, races and cultures, for the endless opportunities of making new relationships, venturing across new frontiers, creating new things, discovering new truths, healing the hurt and the broken.

Forgive us for the narrowness of vision which sees only the clouds and misses the rainbow. Amen

Women of Guatemala, 1993

Reconcile us across barriers

189 Lord, thank you for Jesus,
who removes all the veils of division and oppression.
Forgive us for creating veils which divide us
from one another and from you.
Help us to remove them
and join hands with you and all who serve with you
in the 'unveiling' ministry of liberation.

M Gnanavaram, South India

190 O God ... ease the suspicions that lurk in the back of the mind about
people we cannot see and do not know. Prepare us for a life as full of
unexpected joys as it is of unexpected sorrows.

Thailand

191 Dear Lord, you wanted all people to live in unity and to love each
other. Help us to break down the walls of separation. Break down the
walls of race, colour, creed and language. Make us so that our unity
and love for each other may win many to your fold.

Myanmar

192 Across the barriers that divide race from race:
Across the barriers that divide rich from poor:
Across the barriers that divide people of different faiths:
Reconcile us, O Christ, by your cross.

Based on the prayer 'The Ministry of Reconciliation' by David Cairns

Bridge-builders

193 I think of bridges:
tentative, fragile, too weak for weight
and stress, the first bridge breaks.
So I need more skill in bridging ...
yes, but more hope, for others will break, too.
I need more love if I am to start again,
learning from failure, towards a mid-way meeting.
Bridges begin from both ends
and other people won't start unless they believe I want
to close the gap ...
except that they may have begun from their
end already and I hadn't noticed!
I need more insight, too.

I think of places where bridges must be built:
as people hold dialogue with those of other faiths;
among churches of my own locality;
with those who are made to feel they have no place
in society – hard-drug addicts; alcoholics;
those rejected by family or church, or both.

Make me a builder of bridges, Lord:
help me to listen more and talk less;
to learn, rather than to give advice;
to receive, when I would rather give;
to acknowledge that I do not have all the truth;
to be rejected, hurt and humbled
... and, ever more deeply, to go on loving.

Methodist Church (UK)

Taste and see

194 Taste and see
the sweetness of diversity,
the richness of many cultures
in this one, unique, never uniform,
world.

Taste and see
the bitterness of divisions,
the barrenness of our imaginations,
the false limitations
we put upon the world.

Taste and see
the goodness of creation,
the nourishment of God's giving
in equal love for every child
in the world.

Taste and see
the evil of our denial,
the selfishness of failing to share
with brothers, sisters, resources
of the world.

Creator God
help us to taste and see
welcome and affirm,
celebrate and share –
in the name of Jesus
who came to redeem
the way we live in this world;
in the power of the Spirit,
who, in a world of difference,
makes us one.

Jan S Pickard

Listening to people

195 In the depth of silence
no words are needed,
no language required.
In the depth of silence
I am called to listen ...

Listen to the beating of your heart
Listen to the blowing of the wind,
the movement of the Spirit
Be silent – said the Lord
and know that I am God.

And listen to the cry of the voiceless
Listen to the groaning of the hungry
Listen to the pain of the landless
Listen to the sigh of the oppressed
and to the laughter of children.

For that is authentic communication;
listening to people
living with people
dying for people.

Indonesia

196 I have just hung up; why did he telephone?
I don't know ... Oh! I get it ...
I talked a lot and listened very little.

Forgive me, Lord, it was a monologue and not a dialogue.
I explained my idea and did not get his;
Since I didn't listen, I learned nothing,
Since I didn't listen, I didn't help,
Since I didn't listen, we didn't communicate.

Forgive me, Lord, for we were connected,
and now we are cut off.

Michel Quoist

Seeing one another in a new way

197 Our Father God, Creator of all your different children
all that has come to be has come through you,
lives in your energy,
takes breath because you willed it,
is clothed in your beauty and dignity,
valued and loved by you, Father,
and is part of your world.

Our Father, God, Creator of all your different children,
teach us to love what you have created.
Help us to shed the arrogance that cocoons us
and restricts our growth.
Help us to split the binding threads of self
that we may crawl out into the warmth of your light,
borne on the wings of understanding.

Teach us to see people one by one
and to acknowledge them as our Father's children,
our brothers and sisters:
not to pigeonhole them;
not to hammer them into unnatural moulds
of our own making,
but to rejoice in our differences,

Accepting people as they are
– different but of equal worth –
each one a part of God's creation,
showing something of his love and glory.

Sybil Phoenix

198 God our Mother and Father, be with us as we learn to see one
another with new eyes, hear one another with new hearts, and treat
one another in a new way.

Corrymeela Community

Think again

199 Spirit of Jesus, if I love my neighbour
out of my knowledge, leisure, power or wealth,
help me to understand my neighbour's anger:
the helplessness, that hates my power to help.

And if, when I have answered need with kindness,
my neighbour rises, wakened from despair,
keep me from flinching at the cry for justice
that struggles for the changes that I fear.

If I am hugging safety or possessions,
uncurl my spirit, as your love prevails,
to join my neighbours, work for liberation,
and find my freedom at the mark of nails.

Brian Wren 1973, revised 1994

ONE WORLD – SOLIDARITY IN SUFFERING

`...` ND he shall be called Emmanuel,' a name which means 'God is with us'.

Matthew 1.23 *(Revised English Bible)*

As long as Christ could suffer
– he did suffer and he sorrowed *for* us.
And now that he is risen and can suffer no more
– he suffers *with* us.

Mother Julian of Norwich

Something to do and think about

❖ *The lighting of candles often symbolizes hope in darkness.*

❖ *From the daily press, cut out news items of areas of the world where there is suffering. Read them again and make the experiences and the issues they raise a part of your prayer.*

❖ *In quiet, try to think and feel yourself into these situations. Hold the people in your mind as you pray for them.*

❖ *Write to the mission agency of your Church and/or Christian Aid, and find out how the Church is involved in at least one of these places. Ask if there is some action you can take which will help to alleviate the situation.*

God is with us

200 Lord, you are the giver of life.
In the midst of suffering we celebrate the promise of your peace.
In the midst of oppression, we celebrate the promise of freedom.
In the midst of doubt and despair we celebrate the promise of
faith and hope.
In the midst of fear we celebrate the promise of joy.
In the midst of sin and decay we celebrate the promise of
salvation and renewal.
In the midst of death we celebrate the promise of eternal life.

Christian Conference of Asia

201 Let my tears of joy mingle with the seas –
As I watch entranced by the wonder of Your reign
beneath the ocean flow.
I weep my thanks to You –
As the fisher folk say, 'Let us wait …
let us wait patiently for the sea
to give its bounty.' Amen and Amen!

Jane Ella Montenegro, Philippines

202 O God, our needs are ligatures that bind us to you. Accept at our
hands today this thread of need which runs through the prayers of
your people everywhere, and use it to draw us more closely to you
and to each other, after the example of our Lord and Saviour Jesus
Christ. Amen

John Carden

Beyond the darkness there is light

203 Holy Father,
some day the burden of today's toil,
the goings and comings,
the successes and failures,
the hopes and near despairs,
will all be transformed
into blessed reality! ...

I reach the point of near absurdity:
of thanking you that I live
during the difficult phase
in which hope is still
the beginning of the day!
Day is still struggling,
and has many struggles ahead,
to be born.
From the mingled light and shadow of hope
I greet you, Lord God.

From a Basic Christian Community in the Philippines

204 Beyond the darkness, there is light.
Beyond the griefs and pains of the moment
is the promise of food and freedom for all.

Beyond our current distress is the dream of a tapestry through which
is woven the rainbow colours of truth, freedom, peace and love. And
in the centre of this tapestry is the Son of God who became human
to uphold the Kingdom of justice and righteousness.

Karl Gaspar, Philippines

So much hunger

205 Hunger is a smooth black crow.
Millions of crows
like a black cloud.
O God ...!

Hunger is rebellion.
Is the mysterious force
moving the murderer's knife
in the hand of the poor ...

Hunger is a devil offering dictatorship.
O God!
Hunger is black hands
putting handfuls of alum
into the stomach of the poor.
O God!

We kneel.
Our eyes are Your eyes.
This is Your mouth.
This is Your heart.
And this is Your stomach.
Your stomach hungers, O God.
Your stomach chews alum
and broken glass.

O God!
How nice a plate of rice,
a bowl of soup and a cup of coffee would be.

O God!
Hunger is a crow.
Millions of black crows
like a black cloud
blotting out my view
of Your heaven.

W S Rendra, Indonesia

Commitment to relieve hunger

206 Lord our God,
what should we do?
We cannot personally feed
all your hungry or house your homeless.
Fill our hearts with gratitude
and help us to live more simply,
so that others may simply live.

Sheila Cassidy

207 If the hunger of others is not my own,
If the anguish of my neighbour in all its forms
touches me not,
If the nakedness of my brother
does not torment me,

then I have no reason
to go to church and to live.

Life is this: to love one's neighbour
as oneself;
this is the commandment of God.
Love means deeds, not good wishes.
For this reason I commit myself
to working for the necessities of others.

Javier Torres, Nicaragua

208 Lord, forgive us if we ever complain of compassion fatigue. When
our hearts sink at the sight of so much human suffering, show us
something practical we can do to help in relieving it and give us the
will to do it, for your name's sake. Amen

Pauline Webb

Kumbaya

209 Someone's crying, Lord –
in the casualty department
in the hospital corridors,
in the street,
on the doorstep,
in pain, or loss, or confusion –
Someone's crying, Lord.

Someone's hurting, Lord –
not so anyone can hear or see,
in the secrecy of their home,
in an uncaring community,
their heart is breaking –
Someone's hurting, Lord.

Someone's fighting, Lord –
in Rwanda, in Zaire,
in Haiti, in East Timor,
in Northern Ireland:
angry and distressed,   *(Place names should be changed*
victim and aggressor,   *according to the current news)*
when will it end?
Someone's fighting, Lord.

Someone's praying, Lord –
for the world
and in the world,
sharing tears and tiredness,
offering them in the name of One
who shared our humanity,
who heals our deepest hurts.
Someone's praying, Lord.

Jan S Pickard

Show us how to care

210 Living Lord, we see your tears in the daily news,
appealing to us in helpless, hungry, dehydrated children
and in the bitter anguish of their parents
in Bosnia, the Middle East, in parts of Africa and Asia ...
challenging our complacency through those who are unprotected:
You made us one family:
Lord, show us how to care.

You are Christ, the refugee,
escaping violence and injustice, oppression and war,
earthquake and famine,
seeking asylum, needing shelter, food and clothing
and challenging us to work for peace and justice.
You made us one family:
Lord, show us how to care.

You are Christ, the homeless on our streets.
We pass you by, aware of our guilt but not knowing what to do.
You made us one family:
Lord, show us how to care.

Christ, the prisoner, suffering the humiliation of a prison cell,
longing for release,
for letters and visitors, for words of encouragement and hope,
for acceptance and love,
You made us one family:
Lord, show us how to care.

Christ, you come as the stranger, a newcomer to our town,
and maybe our church;
you come as a visitor from another part of our country
or another part of the world.
You challenge our insularity and prejudice,
our indifference and apathy,
hoping that we shall respond with love and respect,
welcoming you into our fellowship
and with the hospitality of our homes.
You made us one family:
Lord, show us how to care.

Lord Jesus Christ, you are here in our community,
in the sick and house-bound, the bereaved, lonely and depressed,
in the mentally ill and all who are handicapped,
the battered wife and the abused child,
the young person dying of AIDS.
You are unemployed.
You are here, in our midst, longing for our time,
our understanding, our friendship and our love.
You made us one family:
Lord, show us how to care.

Based on Matthew 25.31-46
Maureen Edwards

125

With the offering of our lives

211 O Living God,
as you sustain us in your steadfast mercy,
so inspire in us penitence and courage,
that we may have faith and love and hope enough
as disciples of our Lord Jesus
to hear the cry of the poor
not only with our eyes and our ears,
but with the hospitality of our hearts
and the offering of our lives.
Lord, in your mercy: **Hear our prayer.**

May the Creator encourage us in compassion.
May our Lord Jesus Christ enfold us in his peace.
And may the Holy Spirit set us on fire with praise,
now and forever. Amen

Julie Hulme

Mother love

212 Wrapped in the arms of God's love,
as a child wrapped in a shawl;
fed from God's very being,
as a child nourished at the breast;
resting on the knees of God's love,
as a child leans against the teacher:

Let us pray for the mother,
clutching the child
in wild desperation
as fears of eviction grow.
   Let us pray for the father,
   cradling his son
   in hopeless despair
   as debts mount.
Let us pray for the child,
abused and forlorn,
deprived of love,
no questions answered,
as hatred sets in.

Let us pray for us all:
communities destroyed by monetary policies,
which sacrifice society to individual greed;
organisations capped by economic policies,
which sacrifice compassion to market forces;
countries brought to ruin by their debt to us,
which makes nonsense of our aid to them.

Mother of infinite wisdom,
Christ of infinite compassion,
Holy Spirit, guarantee of change,
bring us to our knees in shame,
bring us to our feet in action,
bring us to our senses in prayer,
that with you we may all inherit
a new heaven and a new earth.

Kate McIlhagga

Lord in your mercy ...

213 O Living God,
we cry out with the poor of the earth,
asking why it is that you seem so far away,
so distant from their anguish.
Lord, in your mercy: **Hear our prayer.**

O God of Justice,
we cry out with the oppressed of the earth:
'Thy Kingdom come!'
Lord, in your mercy: **Hear our prayer.**

O God of all Truth,
we cry out with all those whose voice is unheard,
whose words are silenced,
whose actions are broken,
whose oppression goes unseen or ignored.
Lord, in your mercy: **Hear our prayer.**

O Righteous God,
we cry out with those whose blood is spilt by neighbours,
who suffer from the random viciousness of war,
the planned cruelty of ethnic cleansing.
Lord, in your mercy: **Hear our prayer.**

O God of the Reconciling Cross,
we cry out with all those who are tortured and bereaved
by the nurtured grudges of history,
the malicious ambivalence of the borderlands.
Lord, in your mercy: **Hear our prayer.**

O God of Shalom, we cry out with all those who are denied the fruit
of the labour of their hands,
who endure the slow starvation required by policies made in other
countries,
whose hunger is the wealth of others.
Lord, in your mercy: **Hear our prayer.**

Julie Hulme

For churches that seek justice

214 Give us, O Lord, churches
that will be more courageous than cautious;
that will not merely 'comfort the afflicted'
but 'afflict the comfortable';
that will not only love the world but will also judge the world;
that will not only pursue peace but also demand justice;
that will not remain silent when people are calling for a voice;
that will not pass by on the other side
when wounded humanity is waiting to be healed;
that will not only call us to worship
but also send us out to witness;
that will follow Christ even when the way points to a cross.

To this end we offer ourselves in the name of him who loved us and
gave himself for us. Amen

Christian Conference of Asia

Reconciling love

215 O God of love, most blessed and most holy,
you have given us a message of reconciliation;
a message of love, exemplified in your Son our Lord.

Your love is a special kind of love,
it reaches out to love even the unloving;
it reaches out to us – the broken and sinful.

We celebrate your divine majesty.
We acknowledge your infinite glory.
We praise the wonder of your reconciling love.

Your love is a special kind of love:
it reaches out
    to the neglected and marginalized;
    to the hungry, thirsty and brutalized;
    to single mothers and fatherless children;
    to political prisoners and the distressed;
    to refugees from ethnic cleansing, and the dying.

Your love reaches out to all!

Accept, we pray,
    the adoration of our hearts,
    and reconcile us to you
    and to each other in Jesus' name. Amen

Lesley Anderson, Panama

ONE WORLD –
JUSTICE AND PEACE

N days to come
the mountain of the LORD's house
will be established higher than all other mountains,
towering above other hills.
Peoples will stream towards it;
many nations will go, saying,
'Let us go up to the mountain of the LORD,
to the house of Jacob's God,
that he may teach us his ways
and we may walk in his paths ...'
He will be judge between many peoples
and arbiter among great and distant nations.
They will hammer their swords into mattocks
and their spears into pruning-knives.
Nation will not take up sword against nation;
they will never again be trained for war.
Each man will sit under his own vine
or his own fig tree, with none to cause alarm.
The LORD of Hosts himself has spoken.

Micah 4.1-4 (Revised English Bible)

Something to do and think about

❖ *Find something to symbolize the need for peace (a flower, a piece of barbed wire, a picture, a carving ...) and place it on your worship table.*

❖ *Write a letter of encouragement to someone who has been imprisoned without fair trial. Addresses can be obtained through Amnesty International, 99-119 Rosebury Avenue, London EC1R 4RE (if you live in the UK). Each country has its own branch. Your local Library should be able to find the address for you.*

Blessed are the peacemakers

216 Blessed are the poor ...
not the penniless
but those whose heart is free.

Blessed are those who mourn ...
not those who whimper
but those who raise their voices.

Blessed are the meek ...
not the soft
but those who are patient and tolerant.

Blessed are those who hunger and thirst for justice ...
not those who whine
but those who struggle.

Blessed are the merciful ...
not those who forget
but those who forgive.

Blessed are the pure in heart ...
not those who act like angels
but those whose life is transparent.

Blessed are the peacemakers ...
not those who shun conflict
but those who face it squarely.

Blessed are those who are persecuted for justice ...
not because they suffer
but because they love.

P Jacob, Chile

Make us more just

217 Our Father in heaven,
may your name be held holy,
your kingdom come,
your will be done,
on earth as in heaven.
Give us today our daily bread.
And forgive us our debts,
as we have forgiven those
    who are in debt to us.
And do not put us to the test,
but save us from the Evil One.

Matthew 6.9-13 (New Jerusalem Bible)

218 Lord Jesus Christ,
whose seamless robe of fabric
was exchanged at the cross
for a garment of redeeming blood;
cover, we pray, both believers and nations
with the clothing of your righteousness and justice
that in the hour of judgement
we may behold your glory without shame
and endure your gaze without fear;
for your name's sake. Amen

Norman Wallwork

219 O Lord, who is righteous? Clear thou me from hidden faults.
Let me not exalt myself above others, but let me learn
that humanity walks together through the storm,
that we are all redeemed by good deeds and by thy grace.

Albert Friedlander

That we may do your will

220 Angry Jesus
as of old you entered into that temple market
casting out the merchants and money changers;
enter now into the markets of our modern world.
Throw out of them all that is unworthy, unjust and self-seeking
and direct the market forces of the world
in the ways of justice, plenty and peace,
for your tender mercy's sake. Amen

John Carden

221 God of mercy and hope,
in the struggle for freedom grant us strength;
in decisions about freedom grant us wisdom;
in the practice of freedom grant us guidance;
in the dangers of freedom grant us protection;
in the life of freedom grant us joy
and in the use of freedom grant us vision;
for your name's sake. Amen

Latin American Council of Churches

222 Gracious God ...
Let all be partners in shaping the future
with a faith that quarrels with the present
for the sake of what yet might be.

Taiwan

That we may love your will

223 Dear God, our Father and Mother,
we thank you that you are the God of compassion and justice;
for your promise to turn our darkness into light.
We pray for places where darkness prevails,
for political prisoners who are away from their homelands;
for countries where people experience instability and exploitation
because of the involvement of foreign powers.
We pray that you will bring justice and peace to them.

M Gnanavaram, South India

224 We put our hope in you, Lord of love and mercy.
Rescue us from the cruelty of this world
and bring us to your Kingdom of peace and justice.

Magali do Nascimento, Cunha, Brazil

225 Thank you and praise you for those of every faith tradition ... for the
variety and richness of their spiritualities, for our common quest for
truth, our yearning after love, our longing for peace and
commitment to justice. Ever unite us we pray, help us and inspire us,
that we might live more truly for you throughout our lives. Amen

Week of Prayer for World Peace, 1994

226 God, give us light to know your will,
courage to obey your will
and a heart to love your will.

Nihar Chhatriya, North India

Forgive our silence

227 Lord, forgive us for supporting unjust
and murderous political and religious systems.
Forgive our silence and fear of speaking out.
Give us your grace and strength to act as your children
by working against these life-denying forces.

M Gnanavaram, South India

228 Father, I have often seen power corrupt others –
leaders of armies, industry, governments, churches
and even small family units –
so when you see it happening to me
can you give me a nasty nudge?

Alec Gilmore

229 Give us strength, O Lord,
lightly to bear our joys and sorrows;
love that we may be fruitful in your service
and courage never to disown the poor
or bend our knees to insolent might. Amen

Rabindranath Tagore, India (1861-1941)

Help us in our struggle against evil

230 O God,
uproot in us the love of money,
throwing the poisonous weed
into the fire of your desire.
Harrow our minds
with the sharpness of your truth.
Plant in us the seed of contentment
that we may grow fat with justice
and bring forth peace.

Alison Norris

231 After the night, we pray for dawn.
After war, we pray for peace.
O Lord, fill our hearts with compassion and love,
so that we may walk through the darkness
and emerge into a morning filled with Divine Love.

Albert Friedlander

232 O God of faithful love,
confirm in us the desire to watch with you,
and to be vigilant in the face of evil.

O God of truth,
strengthen in us the courage to stand for what is right,
and to endure the consequences.

O God of peace,
go with us into the places where evil seems triumphant,
and be our faith, hope, love,
so that we may come with you to the resurrection glory
and the triumph of your realm of light.

Julie Hulme

I believe

233 I believe
that women are equal in ability
to men;

I believe
that just because my mother accepted
a subservient role, it does not mean
that I must too;

I believe
that if I do not fight for the rights of my sister,
then she will always be oppressed;

I believe
that limitless horizons lie before my daughter,
not just a few traditional choices;

I believe
that I have much to contribute to the world,
and I alone possess my particular talents and abilities;

I believe
that each woman is an individual,
not a stereotype.

Rene Parmar, Asia

Women and men

234 **Women:** God of justice and righteousness, we come before you pained with the realities of violence, happening within us and around us.

Men: Awaken us to the horror of all violations against life, against women and children, against our own families, against humanity, against creation.

All: Truly we have failed miserably in living as a community. Drive out our carelessness, indifference, wickedness and sinfulness in Jesus name!

Men: We confess our failures, frailties and imperfections including our past acceptance of violence and injustice in relationships between women and men.

Women: We look forward to the future in faith and hope. Working for the day when we, and all our sisters no longer have to fit a stereotype, but are free to use all our gifts and to share in all the benefits of human life and work.

All: We look forward to the age of peace, when violence is banished. Both women and men are able to love and be loved. And the work and wealth of our world is justly shared.

Leader: We look forward to the day when all the peoples of the Earth shall act for equality with all the forces of goodness and love and creative sustainability, that this be our agenda on behalf of our families and the future of our children's children.

Philippines

With Christians in South Africa

235 Throughout the land we stand on the threshold of a new experience of national unity. We are a people composed of many races, many languages, many religious traditions, many political parties, many cultures. We are poor and rich, women and men, young and old. We have emerged from a history of strife and death to seek a future of life and health. We acknowledge the presence of Christ amongst us who reconciles the world.

We struggled against one another: now we are reconciled to struggle for one another.
We believed it was right to withstand one another: now we are reconciled to understand one another.
We endured the power of violence: now we are reconciled to the power of tolerance.

We built irreconcilable barriers between us: now we seek to build a society of reconciliation.
We suffered a separateness that did not work: now we are reconciled to make togetherness work.
We believed we alone held the truth: now we are reconciled in the knowledge that Truth holds us.

We puffed ourselves up to demand others to bow down to us: now we are reconciled to embrace one another in humility before God.
We do not pretend we have already won or are already perfect: now we are reconciled to press on together to the fullness which lies ahead.

We are reconciled to the patience and persistence that makes peace; to the transparency and fairness that makes justice; to the forgiveness and restitution that builds harmony; to the love and reconstruction that banishes poverty and discrimination; to the experience of knowing one another that makes it possible to enjoy one another; to the spiritual strength of the one God, who made us of one flesh and blood, and loves us.

South African Council of Churches, 1994

A Psalm for South Africa

236 Praise the name of the Lord
Praise God who has given us hope!
Praise God, you people living in the land of South Africa
in the streets and farms of our God.

From high blue skies to hot deep mines
from dusty deserts to towering peaks
from grey littered streets to green fields and forests,
From oceans edged with warm white beaches
to concrete cities and long black highways:
The Lord's will is sovereign.

Sing glory to the name of God who inspires hope
Because God has called South Africa to be saved.
We have learned for ourselves that God is great,
that our Lord surpasses all other gods.

The Lord struck down the idols of apartheid,
and denounced pride and racism.
The Lord sent signs and wonders against the false gospel,
and forced change upon its officials ...

O Lord, your name endures for ever!
Lord, Your memory is ever fresh.
For You have vindicated Your children
And honoured those who served God's people ...

South Africa Council of Churches

For peace

237 What kind of world is this
that the adult people are going to leave for us children?
There is fighting everywhere
and they tell us we live in a time of peace.
You are the only one who can help us.
Lord, give us a new world
in which we can be happy
in which we can have friends
and work together for a good future.
A world in which there will not be any cruel people
who seek to destroy us and our world
in so many ways. Amen

A Liberian child

238 O Lord,
remember not only the men and women of good will
but also those of evil will.
But do not remember all the suffering
they have inflicted upon us;
remember the fruits we have borne
thanks to this suffering –
our comradeship, our loyalty, our humility
our courage, our generosity,
the greatness of heart
which has grown out of all this;
and when they come to judgement,
let all the fruits that we have borne
be their forgiveness.

*Germany – This prayer was found scribbled on a piece of wrapping paper
near the body of a dead child at Ravensbruck Concentration Camp*

Let peace fill our world

239 Lead me from Death to Life
from Falsehood to Truth
Lead me from Despair to Hope
from Fear to Trust
Lead me from Hate to Love
from War to Peace
Let Peace fill our Heart
our World, our Universe
Peace – Peace – Peace

This universal prayer for peace has been used since 1981 by people of faith and no faith. Many use it at midday every day.

240 *Before you pray, light a candle*

From the land of the Resurrection and the cradle of the promise of salvation to all humankind through Jesus Christ our Lord, and with a candle of hope, we pray to you, God our Father, that the action of peace-seekers and peace makers may bear fruit so that
Hope will take the place of despair,
Justice will prevail over oppression,
Peace will turn strife into love.

Palestinian Women, Jerusalem

241 All the flowers of tomorrow are in the seeds of today.

Anon – Philippines

Your will be done

242 Lord, teach us to pray.
Be the inspiration of our intercessions,
that we may ask for what you want,
and that our prayers be part of your transforming purposes.

Brian Haymes

243 O God of peace and love,
You came in Jesus as our peace.
You broke down the dividing wall of hostility,
You have shown us that love and peace are practical realities.
Be with us as we count the cost of our responsibilities
to our neighbours far and near. Amen

Akuila Yabaki, Fiji

244 O God of courage, help me
to wrestle out of my despair and restlessness,
and let me know
that only in soothing and empowering
those who are angry and weak
will I ever discover the meaning
of a full life lived with you.

Jane Ella Montenegro, Philippines

245 God of all goodness, grant us ardently to do your will,
wisely to seek it, surely to know it and perfectly to accomplish it,
for the glory of your name.

Thomas Aquinas (1226-1274)

ONE WORLD – GOD'S WORLD

O THE LORD belong the earth and everything in it,
the world and all its inhabitants.
For it was he who founded it on the seas
and planted it firm on the waters beneath.

Psalm 24.1-2 (Revised English Bible)

Something to do and think about

❖ *Try the native American prayer of Six Directions. In unhurried fashion one greets the six directions in prayer.*

246 We turn to the East and face the rising sun – God is praised for the gift of new life, of new days, of youth, of beginnings.

We turn towards the South – we give thanks for those people, events and things which warm our lives and help us to grow and develop.

We turn towards the West where the sun sinks and sets – we praise God for our sunsets, nights, for endings in our lives.

As we face North, we remember the challenges and difficulties in our lives and of our life.

We bend down to touch mother earth, we praise the Creator for the things which sustain our lives.

Finally, we gaze into the sky, we thank God for our hopes and our dreams. Centred in the Creator's universe, we remember God's mighty deeds in our lives and thus move into the future.

Native American

God's design

247 Lord, the whole earth reveals your infinite care
and love for all that your hand fashioned.
You gave form,
light and colour,
depth and shadow
to vast mountains, hills and plains,
skies and clouds,
lakes, rivers, and oceans
and the teeming life that fills them.
You gave birth to sound and music,
the rhythm of winds and seas,
the spontaneity of bird song
and the gentle buzz of insects.
You gave seasons for growth –
the perpetual cycle of decay and resurrection –
life-giving rain,
the warmth of sunshine,
the rich perfume of harvest,
the intricate design of a snowflake
and hoar-frost on a cobweb.
You gave harmony:
the largest and most impressive forms of life
dependent upon the smallest.
Everything demonstrates your wisdom.

The world's infinite variety is your design:
peoples of all languages, nations and cultures,
made in your image,
to discover from one another the breadth of your love
and different facets of your nature.
You made us out of dust,
belonging to the sacred earth from which we came,
to be stewards, using, sharing and preserving
what you provided for the needs of all.

Maureen Edwards

The riches of creation

248 Creator God,
your greatness is seen throughout the earth. We marvel at the infinite detail you give to everything. We thank you for sights which remind us that all life depends on you for birth and continuity.

Who but you, O God, could so faithfully reproduce colour, and design and give shape to every variety of tree, plant and flower?

Who but you, O God, could set before us the magnificence of a landscape refreshed after a shower of rain, or the spectacle of a desert parched by scorching sun?

Who but you, O God, could create the complexity of bird, beast and insect, or the textured diversity of feather, fur or hide?

Lord God, we thank you that over all your dominion, you have fashioned people to savour and experience all the richness of your creation.

Help us always to treat your world with care and sensitivity, as we praise you for your love and goodness to us. Amen

Brenda Armstrong

God sees the sparrow fall

249 These words are written at a window
overlooking a back-yard
on the industrial edge of a great city.
The sounds of heavy traffic, by road and rail, planes overhead,
power drills, TV laughter and electronic music,
almost drown the song of a blackbird on the chimney pot.

There is a layer of grime on the sill,
the air is heavy with fumes,
yet in the yard grow roses and marigolds, geraniums and herbs.
Blades of grass burst through the cracks of the paving,
green leaves breathe a fresher air.

People are at work, at odds with each other,
anxious about their jobs, health, housing,
they are angry and afraid –
they do not have time to stand and see
a sparrow ruffle its feathers in the sunlight on the wall.
But God sees the sparrow fall – and fly –
and on the wasteland thistles,
a charm of goldfinches.

God, our Creator, you daily rise in hope upon this imperfect world.
May we see your creation with new eyes, and live that hope:
'Daystar in our hearts appear!'

Jan S Pickard

In penitence

250 I am ashamed before the earth;
I am ashamed before the heavens;
I am ashamed before the evening twilight;
I am ashamed before the blue sky;
I am ashamed before the darkness;
I am ashamed before the sun;
I am ashamed before the One standing
within me who speaks to me.

The Navaho, Canadian Indian

251 Dear Father, we celebrate your mighty acts,
your wonderful work in creation.
The more scientists delve into nature,
the more of that marvellous order is revealed –
the symmetry and balance –
the evidence of your hand at work is overwhelming.
We wonder, we praise, we thank you.

And yet, dear Father,
so often we fail to live up to the goodness
which is in all that you have made.
We abuse your creation for our own selfish motives;
we fail to love our neighbours,
or to let you into the deep dark places within us.
We are truly sorry and ask your forgiveness.

You are a merciful God,
and we know we can turn to you full of sorrow
and be redeemed.
Enter now into our lives and fill us with your Spirit
so that we may be truly your people: in the name of Christ. Amen

Andrew East

Restoring lost images

252 We confess –
that we have considered the earth to be our own,
believing God gave us dominion, and thus absolute control
over it.

We affirm –
'the earth is the Lord's and all that is in it,
for he has founded it on the seas
and established it on the rivers' (Psalm 24.1-2).

We repent –
we know we need to change our understanding of creation,
taking our share of responsibility for its care and protection.

We believe –
that the Spirit, God's recreating power, is active in us and in the
world.

God, Creator of all,
may humankind be freed from the greed
which is destroying the earth;
and may your churches be courageous
in taking up causes against the forces that threaten life. Amen

Akuila Yabaki, Fiji

253 Lord, help us to work with you
in restoring the lost, but beautiful, images
of your creation
and bring them back to you.

M Gnanavaram, South India

Restoring our humanity

254 Great Spirit, whose dry lands thirst, help us to find the way to refresh your lands.
We pray for your power to refresh your lands.
Great Spirit, whose waters are choked with debris and pollution, help us to find a way to cleanse your waters.
We pray for your knowledge to find the way to cleanse the waters.
Great Spirit, whose beautiful earth grows ugly with misuse, help us to find the way to restore the beauty of your handiwork.
We pray for the strength to restore the beauty of your handiwork.
Great Spirit, whose creatures are being destroyed, help us to find the way to replenish them.
We pray for the power to replenish the earth.
Great Spirit, whose gifts to us are being lost in selfishness and corruption, help us to find the way to restore our humanity.
We pray for your wisdom to find the way to restore our humanity.

Great Spirit,
Give us hearts to understand
Never to take from creation's beauty
More than we give;
Never to destroy wantonly
For the furtherance of greed;
Never to deny to give our hands
For the building of earth's beauty;
Never to take from her
What we cannot use.

Give us hearts to understand
That to destroy earth's music
Is to create confusion;
That to wreck her appearance
Is to blind us to beauty;
That to pollute her fragrance
Is to poison the air we breathe.

That as we care for her
She will care for us.

American Indian women

Commitment to nurture the earth

255 We commit ourselves
To join with you, O God
To nurture
The plants and animals,
The elements,
The sacred womb of sea and soil.
We offer you our ability to create and
Our potential to release
People's loving energies
For the benefit of all creation.
We sing with you the song of the universe!
We dance with you the dance of life!
We are yours,
And you in us are hope
For the renewing of nature
Through the healing of the nations.

Salvador Martinez, Thailand

I believe

256 I believe, Lord,
that everything good in the world
comes from you.
I believe in your great love for all people.
I believe that, because you preached love,
freedom and justice,
you were humiliated,
tortured and killed.

I believe that you continue
to suffer in our people ...
I believe that you call me
to defend your cause,
but I also believe that you accompany me
in the task of transforming this world
into a different one
where there is no suffering or weeping;
a world where there is a gigantic table
set with free food
where everyone is welcome.

I believe that you accompany us
in waiting for the dawning of a new day.
I believe that you will give us strength
so that death does not find us
without having done enough,
and that you will rise
in those who have died seeking a different world.

A peasant woman, El Salvador

We want a world renewed

257 I believe in the equality of all,
rich and poor.
I believe in liberty.
I believe in humanity and that through it
we can create unity.
I believe in the love within each of us,
and in the home, happy and healthy.
I believe in the forgiveness of our sins.
I believe that with divine help
we will have the strength to establish
equality in society.
I believe in unity, the only way to
achieve peace, and I believe that
together we can obtain justice.

Ayacucho youth group, Peru

258 O God of all youth, we pray to you:
We are young people, and we want to celebrate life!
We cry out against all that kills life:
    hunger, poverty, unemployment, sickness,
    repression, individualism, injustice.
We want to announce fullness of life:
    work, education, health, housing,
    bread for all.
We want a communion, a world renewed,
We hope against hope.
With the Lord of history we want to make all things new.

Group of Brazilian young people

For healing and unity

259 Let us pray for the peace of the world:
that nations and peoples, communities and individuals, may learn to
understand one another, to respect and honour one another,
   and to trust one another;
that those in authority in this and every land may govern in
   accordance with God's will, seeking justice for all.
Lord of the present, the past and the future
We bring you our prayers, our love and our lives.

Let us pray for the beauty of the world:
that human skills and inventiveness may be harnessed to enhance
   and not destroy it;
that artists, writers, musicians, those of great talent and amateurs
   alike, may have opportunity to enrich it;
that every eye and ear may be opened to enjoy it.
Lord of the present, the past and the future
We bring you our prayers, our love and our lives.

Let us pray for the health of the world:
for those who work to overcome disease and malnutrition
   and insanitary living conditions;
for those who minister to the suffering, the friendless
   and the needy;
for those with physical or mental disabilities;
for drug addicts and alcoholics;
for those who suffer pain, and for those who wantonly inflict pain,
that they may be healed.
Lord of the present, the past and the future
We bring you our prayers, our love and our lives.

Let us pray for the faith of the world:
that those who see no meaning in life
may be brought to an understanding of God's purposes,
and to put their trust in God's leading;
and that those who are committed to God's service
may live in unity,
and witness to the gospel of Christ by our word
   and our example.
Lord of the present, the past and the future
We bring you our prayers, our love and our lives.

John Pritchard

155

I have seen the Lord

260 Where the mist rises from the sea,
Where the waves creep upon the shore,
Where the wrack* lifts upon the strand,
    I have seen the Lord.

Where the sun awakens the day,
Where the road winds on its way,
Where the fields are sweet with hay,
    I have seen the Lord.

Where the stars shine in the sky,
Where the streets so peaceful lie,
Where the darkness is so nigh,
    I have seen the Lord.

The Lord is here,
The Lord is there,
The Lord is everywhere.
The Lord is high,
The Lord is low,
The Lord is on the path I go.

In the Celtic tradition, David Adam

* 'wrack' (Scottish) – seaweed

Hoping for a world renewed

261 I believe that life is great!

I believe in young people,
the hope of tomorrow.

I believe in truth and justice.

I am praying for young people
because life is great
and you deserve to live it.

I want to drink a toast with you
to your life as an adult.

Everything is possible for you,
the worst and the best.

I believe that young people
will win through
and form a new and better humanity.

Prayer of an Ayacucho youth group, Peru

262 Lord, we don't think of ourselves as rich people,
but many in the world would stand amazed at what we possess.
Help us to accept the good things we have with thanksgiving,
but let them not take over our lives.
Open our eyes to the needs of others,
open our hearts to love and care,
open our hands that we may not grasp your bounty to ourselves,
but share it with others.

Jesus said, 'Give to everyone who asks you ...'
Help us to know that in giving we serve you. Amen

Val Spouge

Stars

263 Visa card, sky-high bills,
Run-down mother popping pills.
Paper homes, shivering limbs,
Colder, colder, bright eyes dimmed ...
Stiff back ... propped with hope
Now crouched and crashed, smashed on dope.
Fish floating on frothy oceans,
Fed on chemicals, devoid of motion.
Classic buildings, fallen rubble,
This war, that war, endless trouble.
Hopeless, hopeful bundles of words
Trying to solve things – how absurd,
When bombs explode a hard-won trust
Peace collapses under the lust
Of desperate men with narrow vision,
No love, no God, or too much religion?

In each direction ... no way out!
With each reflection – I can't cope.

Wait a minute!
Pause to think
Of nothing, into reverie sink ...
Let smooth silence hold you,
The milky sunset bathe your mind,
Dancing stars caress your eyes.
And you will find
Sometimes the world doesn't need you
And can be left behind.

Alison Mann, Questors Youth Club, Wolverhampton

ONE WORLD - THE WORLD CHURCH

, the prisoner of the Lord, urge you therefore to lead a life worthy of the vocation to which you were called. With all humility and gentleness, and with patience, support each other in love. Take every care to preserve the unity of the Spirit by the peace that binds you together. There is one Body, one Spirit, just as one hope is the goal of your calling by God. There is one Lord, one faith, one baptism, and one God and Father of all, over all, through all and within all.

Ephesians 1.1-6 (New Jerusalem Bible)

Something to do and think about

❖ *Write a letter of greeting to another part of the World Church, expressing solidarity with fellow Christians there. Your minister may be able to help you with the address.*

We are invited

264 Lord Jesus Christ,
we love to celebrate
the joy of weddings,
birthdays and success ...
to meet around a table and share food and news,
to give and receive presents.
You said the Kingdom of God is like that!
Here and now,
people of every race and age-group
are set free by your cross,
forgiven, liberated from selfishness,
prejudice and insularity.
People from every part of the world
are released from all that divides and separates
to form a new community,
enjoying one another's company,
listening to and receiving from one another
at the great feast God prepared.

Never before have there been such opportunities
for meeting and being enriched
by the infinite variety God has given.
Yet, you reminded us
of those who declined the invitation!
Preoccupied with property, possessions,
their own little world – even family life –
'We haven't time!' they said.

Teach us to make time
to go on building up relationships
with all who are invited
to celebrate God's feast.

Based on Luke 14.16-24, Maureen Edwards

Guests at God's banquet

265 We thank thee, our king, for a new day,
For a new pouring forth of thy wine of life,
For a new bidding to thy feast,
To the eternal triumph-banquet of thy kingdom,
Wherein we on earth and thy beloved in heaven,
May conjointly be glad and rejoice,
Sharing the divine revelry,
The melody, the rapture of perfect delight.

Give us, we pray thee, the simplicity and purity of little children,
That, nothing questioning, we may gather gladly,
With thy whole family in heaven and earth,
Round this thy table of a new day.
Make thin, O Lord, make very thin the veil
Which divideth us who are yet in the flesh
From those others, our fellow-guests,
Who feast with us, unseen by our outward eyes,
But to be beheld how wondrously,
In what clear glory of deathless perfection,
When thou dost enlighten the eyes of our spirit,
With the eternal radiance of thine own presence.

For fitness to be guests at God's banquet:
a prayer written for use in an Indian college

266 Thank you Heavenly Father
for bringing me into such a special worldwide family.

Zaire

We confess

267 O Lord, our God,
we confess with shame
that our prejudices have created
barriers between ourselves and others.
We let age, race, colour, and gender,
   religion, economics, nationalism and cultural background
   disentangle us – your people.
We have marred the image of your Church
   and massacred your body afresh.
We see again the cross, your sweat, the nails,
   your blood!
We hear your voice – challenging us
   to become more like you.
We see your arms outstretched – beckoning us
   to come into your loving embrace.

Yet we remain victims of our own prejudices –
   chained to the walls of oppression and shame.
We have fear-filled assumptions about others –
   people who are ... yes, different!
We have misinformed feelings about the homeless,
   the suffering poor, the marginalized, victims of AIDS,
We have an ignorant apathy towards handicapped people.
We oppress others by isolating them.
We put walls between 'them' and 'us'.
What have we done to your Church, O Lord?

Lord, you are a friend of all,
   Forgive us that we failed you.
   Forgive us that we have failed others.
   Forgive us that we have failed to recognize
   the pain of our oppression
   and grant that we may now experience the many ways
   others can enrich our lives. Amen

Lesley Anderson, Panama

We are forgiven

268 Brothers and sisters, in the presence of the God of glory,
We need to confess our true human condition.
In the light of Christ's self-giving life,
    his way of the Cross,
We see the darkness in our lives.
(Silence as we reflect on the life of the individual)

As we think of the evil and oppression in the world
    of which we are a part,
We need to repent together with our fellow-humans.
(Silence as we reflect on the world's life)

As members of a people called to follow Christ
and live in his new righteousness,
We need to repent for the evil in the Church's life.
(Silence as we reflect on the life of the Church)

The Saviour of the world, the Refuge of the repentant,
forgives and strengthens all who truly seek his grace.
He accepts you as his sons and daughters,
and sets you free from the bondage of your past.
For Christ died and rose to new life that we might all share his
wholeness and abundant life. Amen

Church of South India

269 Let your kingdom come, O Lord, into our churches, into our praying,
into our singing, into our hearts, into our hands, and into our eyes;
through Christ our Lord. Amen

Czech Liturgy

Enable us to be a people of praise

270 God, you can work miracles
with one or two faithful people.

A remnant Church
reformed and renewed
by your Spirit
can do a mighty work
to represent your future
and proclaim your judgement and forgiveness.

Forgive us
for imagining you are always on the side
   of the big battalions;
for believing that strength can be identified
   with big crowds and growing numbers,
   with overflowing collections and slick organisation.

Help us to be very wary
of those who claim to speak your word
because they point to sensational victories
and attract a wide-eyed following.

Rather we praise you
for your remnant prophets,
lonely people like Elijah, Hosea and Jeremiah,
controversial ones like Luther, Romero and Tutu
and the nameless saints ...

Above all, our thoughts are of Jesus:
humanity's cast-off, crucified and rejected,
eternal sign of your power in a solitary life.
Through him work your miracle of mercy
and enable us to allow his obedience to lead us
to be a people of praise.

David Jenkins

We commit ourselves

271 We commit ourselves to deepen our inner lives
so that we will not fear the future.
We commit ourselves to renounce private forms of faith,
to live in communities of support and affirmation.
We commit ourselves to the way of non-violence,
cherishing forgiveness and reconciliation,
being prepared to suffer for the Kingdom.
We commit ourselves to develop solidarity
with our sisters and brothers in every land
who share with us the dream of shalom.
We commit ourselves to light candles in the dark,
to speak when all around are silent,
and to live the gospel in simplicity.
We commit ourselves to celebrate the promise of peace,
to nurture the spirit of festivity
and to grow in joy and expectation.
Alleluia!

Christian Conference of Asia

272 Lord God
whose Son was content to die
to bring new life,
have mercy on your church
which will do anything you ask,
anything at all,
except die
and be reborn.

Ian Fraser

For healing and unity

273 Lord God, we give thanks for our rich diversity
within the community of faith.
Teach us mutual respect in issues where we differ,
and to rejoice in the living presence
of Christ the shepherd
who makes us one.

Leta Hawe, New Zealand

274 Lord,
make us realize that our Christianity is like a rice field:
when it is newly planted the paddies are prominent,
but as the plants take root and grow taller
these divided paddies gradually vanish
and soon there appears only one vast continuous field.

So give us roots that love
and help us grow in Christian fellowship and service
that thy will be done in our lives
through our Saviour, Jesus Christ.

Philippines

275 O God,
who out of your great love
gave Jesus to the world,
by a glad exchange of concern and prayer across the world
help us to be bearers and sharers of that same love,
for love's sake.

John Carden

Build us into one Church

276 O God, the Creator and Father of all humankind,
by your Holy Spirit you have made a diversity of peoples one
in the confession of your name.
Lead us, we pray, by the same Spirit
to display to the whole earth one mind in belief
and one passion for righteousness;
through Jesus Christ our Lord.

Church of South India

277 Gather us and scatter us, O God,
according to your will.
Build us into one church,
a church with open doors and large windows,
a church which takes the world seriously,
ready to work and to suffer
and even to bleed for it,
as we follow and witness to him
who is the Saviour of the World,
Jesus Christ, our Lord. Amen

Eastern Europe

278 O Lord our God ...
You accept the prayers of our sisters and brothers
In Africa, Asia, Australia, America and Europe.
We are all one in prayer.
So may we, as one, rightly carry out your commission
To witness and to love
In the Church and throughout the world.
Accept our prayers graciously,
Even when they are somewhat strange.
They are offered in Jesus' name.

Ghana

Bread for community

279 God, food of the poor;
Christ our bread,
give us a taste of the tender bread
from your creation's table;
bread newly taken
from your heart's oven,
food that comforts and nourishes us.
A fraternal loaf that makes us human
joined hand in hand,
working and sharing.
A warm loaf that makes us a family;
sacrament of your body,
your wounded people.

Workers in community soup kitchens in the shanty towns of Lima, Peru.

280 Blessed are you, Creator of this earth,
we praise you for the gifts we have received,
so frail and insecure do we become,
we need the peace and strength which your love gives.

Bread and wine, O God we bring to you,
Source of life, we pray for peace and harmony.

Blessed are you, sustainer of our world,
you give to us your freedom and salvation.
May these works of loving human hands
be food and drink for all your holy people.

Brazil

ACKNOWLEDGMENTS AND SOURCES

We are grateful for permission to use material from publishers listed below. While every effort has been made to trace copyright owners, we apologize for any rights which have been inadvertently overlooked.

Asia Women's Resource Centre for Culture and Theology – 3

Booth, Howard *Seven Whole Days* (published by Arthur James Ltd 1992) – 52

Brazilian Bishops Conference – 280

CAFOD – *Celebrating One World* – 64
    2 'Prayer of the Incas' – quoted by Eduardo Galeano in *Genesis – Memory of Fire* (Minerva 1990) and again by CAFOD in *Continent of Hope*

Cambridge University Press – *Book of Common Prayer* – 51
    (Gregorian Sacramentary), the rights in which are vested in the Crown. Reproduced by permission of the Crown's Patentee, Cambridge University Press

Oxford University and Cambridge University Press 1989 *Revised English Bible*

Chelmsford Diocesan House of Retreat – 105

Christian Aid – *Companions of God – Praying with Christians in the Holy Land,* Janet Morley 1994 – 89, 91
    Invitation to Life 1994 – 11

Christian Conference of Asia – 164, 200, 205, 214, 271
    Caring for God's Creation: Asia Sunday 1993 Liturgy – 17, 255
    Your Will be Done – 233, 274

Church Missionary Society (CMS) – 68, 85, 174
    Morning Noon and Night, edit. John Carden – 45, 132, 145, 265

Church of South India – 72, 268, 276

Collins *Heart of Prayer,* edit. Anthony Gittins – 102

Columban House – *Prayers from a Columban House,*
    edit. Peter Millar, Scotland – 56, 100, 114, 128, 272

Cosnett, Elizabeth © – 185

Comision Episcopal de Accion Social, Lima Peru – 257, 261 *Permission sought*

Corrymeela Community – 120,
    Worshipping Together – 198

Claretian Publications, Philippines – *How Long? Prison Reflections of Karl Gaspar* – 204 *Permission sought*

Darton Longman and Todd – *The Broken Body,* Jean Vanier – 154
    New Jerusalem Bible Pages 23 and 113 (published and copyright 1985 by Darton Longman and Todd Ltd. and Doubleday & Co. Inc., and used by permission of the publishers)

Penguin Books / Pelican – *Daily Prayer, edit.* Eric Milner-White
and G W Briggs – 46, 122, 170

Philippine Ecumenical Network (PEN) – 36, 148, 150, 179, 203

Phoenix, Sybil *With all my love* – 197

SCM Press *Letters and Papers from Prison* 1971 edition – 156
Epilogues and Prayers, William Barclay 125

Seremane, Joe, South Africa – 126 *Permission sought*

Society for the Propagation of Christian Knowledge (SPCK) –
All Desires Known, Janet Morley 1992 – 53, 131, 149, 161
Another Day, edit. John Carden – 104, 147
Edge of Glory, David Adam – 127
Jerusalem Prayers, George Appleton – 25
My God My Glory, Eric Milner-White – 76
One Man's Prayers, George Appleton – 20, 42, 79
Tides and Seasons, David Adam – 82, 96, 158, 260

South Africa Council of Churches – 235, 236

Selly Oak, Department of Mission – Prayer used during a conference
held under the auspices of the Department of Mission, the Selly Oak
Colleges, in 1992 – 187

St Andrews Press *Worship Now,* David Cairns – 192

United Church Board for World Ministries From *Calendar of Prayer
1986-1987* – 258

United Church of Christ in the Philippines – *The United Church Letter* – 234

United Reformed Church (UK) *Prayer Handbooks:*
1986 – *The Word and the World* – 58, 270
1987 – *The Power and the Glory* – 216
1994 – *Edged with Fire 1994* – 35, 118, 139, 178, 190, 222
1993 – *The Encompassing Presence* – 173, 212

United Society for the Propagation of the Gospel (USPG) *Transmission* – 250

Week of Prayer for World Peace – 225

Wild Goose Publications – *The Iona Worship Book* – 110, 177, 278

Women's World Day of Prayer Palestine Committee – 90, 240

Women's World Day of Prayer (UK) – 188, 254

World Council of Churches, Geneva, Switzerland – 195
Consultation on Sharing the Cross-cultural Richness of the Gospel,
Chicago, May 1994 – 18
With all God's People – 32, 258
Canberra Assembly 1991 – 19, 23

INDEX OF FIRST LINES

176

INDEX OF SUBJECTS